Breaking Free

Breaking Free
How To Stop Gambling

A Workbook

Edited by

Professor Henrietta Bowden-Jones OBE
National Problem Gambling Clinic, London

Dr. Venetia Leonidaki
National Problem Gambling Clinic, London

CAMBRIDGE
UNIVERSITY PRESS

University Printing House, Cambridge CB2 8BS, United Kingdom

One Liberty Plaza, 20th Floor, New York, NY 10006, USA

477 Williamstown Road, Port Melbourne, VIC 3207, Australia

314–321, 3rd Floor, Plot 3, Splendor Forum, Jasola District Centre,
New Delhi – 110025, India

103 Penang Road, #05–06/07, Visioncrest Commercial, Singapore 238467

Cambridge University Press is part of the University of Cambridge.

It furthers the University's mission by disseminating knowledge in the pursuit of
education, learning, and research at the highest international levels of excellence.

www.cambridge.org
Information on this title: www.cambridge.org/9781911623922
DOI: 10.1017/9781911623946

© The Royal College of Psychiatrists 2022

First published 2022

Printed in the United Kingdom by TJ Books Limited, Padstow Cornwall

A catalogue record for this publication is available from the British Library.

ISBN 978-1-911-62392-2 Paperback

Contents

Downloadable pdfs of the worksheets can be found in the resources tab at
www.cambridge.org/breakingfree

Acknowledgements

To Nancy.

This manual is dedicated to Professor Nancy Petry, one of the greatest addiction psychologists of our time who died prematurely ten years after I founded the National Problem Gambling Clinic.

Her early research into the treatment of gambling disorder using cognitive behavioural techniques was the foundation upon which we built this manual.

Her generous, instructive encouragement as I embarked on the task of setting up the first and only National Health Service gambling disorder clinic in the UK in 2008 was something for which I will be forever grateful.

Nancy died in 2018. She was due to be one of the authors of this manual which is the product of fifteen years of work at the National Problem Gambling Clinic treating thousands of patients suffering from gambling harm

At the last count, over two hundred and fifty psychologists and psychiatrists have worked at our clinic, it is from myself, as the founder and director and from all of these colleagues as well as the thousands of treated patients and their families that I would like to dedicate 'Breaking Free: How to Stop Gambling" to Nancy.

A special thank you also to Dr Venetia Leonodaki, our Lead Consultant Clinical psychologist who took on the task of bringing together and organising this manual into the final version needed for publication.

Prof Henrietta Bowden-Jones OBE.

Contributors

Professor Henrietta Bowden-Jones OBE is the Founder and Director of the National Problem Gambling Clinic, the UK's first NHS clinic set up specifically to treat Gambling Disorders. She is spokesperson on Behavioural Addictions for the Royal College of Psychiatrists and President of Psychiatry at the Royal Society of Medicine. She was awarded an OBE in the 2019 New Year's Honours for services to Addiction Treatment and Research.

Jenny Cousins is a Systemic Practitioner and Humanistic Integrative Counsellor, with over fifteen years' experience in the NHS as well as voluntary and private settings. Since 2006 she has worked in a number of NHS Addictions services, providing therapy to people and their families dealing with a range of addictions including drugs, alcohol, and gambling. She set up and developed the family services at the National Problem Gambling Clinic and continues in her role as Family Lead while completing the training to become a Systemic Psychotherapist.

Zoe Delaney worked as an Assistant Psychologist at the National Problem Gambling Clinic in London, UK. A key feature of her role was supporting individuals at the Clinic in preparing to change their problematic gambling and implement stimulus control strategies. Zoe has worked for the NHS for for over five years and has a Master's degree in Affective Disorders from King's College London.

Andre Geel is a Chartered and Consultant Clinical Psychologist and an Associate Fellow of the British Psychological Society. He is Lead Psychologist for Addictions in a large NHS Trust in London. He was previously Chair of the Faculty of Addictions for the British Psychological Society. He has published in community, general, and addictions psychology. He has been advisor to the National Institute for Clinical Excellence on a number of occasions, lectures, and supervises in Clinical Psychology on a number of Doctorate-level university courses, and has presented at numerous national and international conferences.

Rebecca Harris is a Systemic Family Psychotherapist and manager, with over twenty years' experience in the NHS as well as voluntary and private settings. Since 2004 she has worked in a number of NHS Addictions services, providing both inpatient and community therapy to people and their families dealing with a wide range of addictions including drugs, alcohol, 'chemsex', and behavioural disorders. Rebecca is currently the Senior Manager at the National Problem Gambling Clinic in Central and North West London NHS Foundation Trust. She also manages the newly established National Centre for Gaming Disorders and the innovative Club Drug Clinic.

Professor Ryan Kemp is a Consultant Clinical Psychologist and currently Director of Therapies in Central & North West London NHS Foundation Trust. He is Honorary Professor of Clinical Practice at Brunel University London and associate fellow of the British Psychological Society. Ryan was an early team member in National Problem Gambling Clinic and has worked and researched in the addiction field for more than twenty years. His first book, *Transcending Addiction*, was published by Routledge in 2018.

Dr Venetia Leonidaki is a Consultant Clinical Psychologist at the National Problem Gambling Clinic and a chartered member of the British Psychological Society. She is an accredited supervisor with the British Association for Behavioural and Cognitive Psychotherapies and an accredited Dynamic Interpersonal Therapist with the British Psychoanalytic Council. She teaches regularly about addiction, mental health, and psychotherapy. She has published in peer-reviewed journals and presented in conferences. She sees clients both in the NHS and private practice.

Annika Lindberg is a Chartered Counselling Psychologist who practises in London, UK. She has specialised in gambling addiction since 2004 and first spent a few years living in Las Vegas conducting research and clinical treatment for this client group. She joined the National Problem Gambling Clinic in London UK as one of the first clinicians when they opened their doors in 2010. Since leaving in 2012, she has run treatment and education programmes for gamblers and clinicians. Annika is a Trustee on the board of the Gordon Moody Association, a UK-based inpatient rehab for severely affected addicted gamblers.

Georgina Luck has been an Assistant Psychologist in a variety of mental health services for the past three years and has a Master's degree in Clinical Psychology. Georgina conducts assessments and delivers intervention for problem gamblers and their families, both individually and in groups, at the National Problem Gambling Clinic. Her interests include how best to involve family members and carers in psychological treatment and how to support them in addition to working with clients individually.

Antony Malvasi is a Chartered Counselling Psychologist registered with the British Psychological Society and Health and Care Professions Council. He is passionate about helping people free themselves from their addiction and has extensive experience using CBT and psychodynamic therapy in the treatment of drug, alcohol, and gambling addiction in the NHS and private practice. He is currently working as a senior psychologist and supervisor at the National Problem Gambling Clinic.

Dolors Manuel-Riu is a Senior Clinical Psychologist at the National Problem Gambling Clinic, specialising in CBT, and a chartered member of the British Psychological Society. She has twenty years of experience working in substance misuse and mental health settings in the NHS. In the last nine years, she has specialised in treating gambling disorder. She is a registered motivational interviewing (MI) trainer and regularly provides MI training for NHS staff. She has also provided training on the topics of gambling and addiction to various audiences, including primary care and NHS addiction services, university courses, and via the British Psychological Society and Housing Associations.

Professor Amanda Roberts is part of the Psychology Department at the University of Lincoln. She holds a PhD in Behavioural Neuroscience from Cardiff University. She has numerous multidisciplinary collaborations including an honorary research contract at the National Problem Gambling Clinic and a Research Fellowship at the Gambling Addictions Research Centre, Auckland University of Technology, New Zealand. Amanda's research interests include the evaluation of gambling addiction treatment programmes, both in the community and in UK prisons, and additional interests extend across topics that relate to gambling comorbidity, gambling in vulnerable populations, and gambling and interpersonal violence.

Dr Emmert Roberts is a clinical academic and practising addictions psychiatrist. He graduated with distinctions in medicine from the University of Oxford, Epidemiology from the the London School of Hygiene and Tropical Medicine and holds a PhD in Addiction Sciences from King's College London". He is a member of both the Royal Colleges of Physicians and Psychiatrists, and has a strong interest in substance misuse, co-morbidity, and overall physical and mental health conditions.

Dr Frank Ryan was trained as a Clinical Psychologist at Edinburgh University. He works as a cognitive behaviour therapist with a special interest in addiction. He is a visiting Research Fellow at London South Bank University and an Honorary Senior Lecturer at Imperial College Faculty of Medicine. His research interests include motivation and cognition, especially in the context of addiction.

Dr Steve Sharman is an academic researcher who specialises in gambling behaviour. He has a PhD in Experimental Psychology from the University of Cambridge, where his thesis explored cognitive distortions and decision-making in gambling behaviour. He is a current Society for the Study of Addiction (SSA) Griffith Edwards Academic Fellow at the University of East London, where he uses Virtual Reality to research gambling behaviour. Steve is also a Research Fellow (Gambling Studies) at the National Addiction Centre, King's College London, where he works closely with the National Problem Gambling Clinic.

1 Introduction

Venetia Leonidaki

Gambling addiction is a powerful habit and its impact is often destructive for the individual gambling and those around him/her. Its addictive nature can lead to significant debts, severe anxiety and depression, relationship breakdown, social isolation, stress in families, loss of employment, criminal activities, and, tragically, suicide. As with any addictive behaviour, Gambling addiction creates an internal conflict. An individual gambling problematically may veer between wanting to quit gambling once and for all and succumbing to the urge to place another bet.

Saying goodbye to gambling is not easy. If it were, we would have never needed to write this book in the first place. A key feature of addictive behaviours is that people continue with their habit even after they realise that it is damaging and should be stopped. This tension causes frustration and confusion. It affects people's view of themselves and their relationships with their loved ones.

The truth is that breaking free of old habits is never simple. Behavioural science, the study of human and animal behaviour, explains that when a habit is formed, it becomes second nature. Indeed, human beings are creatures of habit and 45% of our daily activities are habitual. Our brain favours habits because when we are in familiar territory and do things automatically, we rely on existing knowledge to save mental energy. Habits help us enormously in living our life efficiently and are an ingrained part of human nature.

Because they are deeply ingrained in human nature, habits, including addictions, are extremely hard to break. The opposite is also true. Adopting new habits, such as daily exercise or eating healthily, can be equally challenging, even when we know that these behaviours will ultimately benefit us. If humans did not struggle with adopting new habits or breaking old ones, we would not be in need of coaches, trainers, dieticians or psychologists. The fact that there is a need for these professions is the ultimate proof of how challenging changing our habits really is.

The rewarding nature of gambling also contributes to its addictive quality. The occasional wins in gambling promote the false belief that all one needs to do to receive a huge reward at the end is to persevere with the gambling. The environment around us further encourages the gambling behaviour via constant reminders, making gambling hard to forget even if we try. Being regularly exposed to gambling-related reminders, such as adverts on the TV or betting shops in the high street, will automatically bring up memories of past gambling and feelings of excitement and arousal, which fuel the desire to gamble further. This process is often so automatic that we do not always come to realise that our brain and body are affected and driven by seemingly innocent reminders.

Addictive habits can also form coping strategies for dealing with underlying emotional pain. Gambling then becomes a form of distraction, numbing the pain associated with negative memories and self-critical judgements. Our culture is another factor contributing to the addictive nature of gambling. We live in a culture of excess that bombards us with the message that what we own determines our worth and makes us believe that money is the key to happiness. Thus, when we consider all the above, it is far from surprising that trying to break free from gambling can feel like an ordeal. Hopefully this book will offer some help and, at the very least, will be a good starting point for tackling your gambling habit.

Who Is This Workbook For?

This workbook is primarily written for individuals affected by gambling-related harms and readers whose gambling habit has become addictive in nature. You may be reading this workbook because you have decided to take action to break free from your gambling or because you have contemplated doing so. The following chapters will guide you through a number of practical exercises that could help you drop your gambling habit. The points of each chapter that are most pertinent for skill practice are summarised at the end of each chapter.

This workbook is also written for the significant others of those affected by gambling-related harms. Behind every person affected by gambling-related harms, there is a hidden group of people who are also affected: their spouse/partner, children, parents and friends. If you belong to this group, we hope that reading this book helps you act as a co-therapist and support your loved one with the skill practice described in this book or simply understand more about gambling and its treatment before you initiate a conversation with your loved one. At the end of each chapter, we capture the points that are most relevant to significant others. Chapter 14 directly addresses significant others and focuses on how they can support themselves while they try to support their loved ones.

Finally, we have written this book for clinicians treating individuals affected by gambling-related harms. This workbook describes a particular set of skills that could help you structure your treatment course. The exercises in the following chapters could be shared with your clients in therapy or be handed out to them to read between sessions. Of course, depending on each individual client, adaptation of the material may be necessary to match the client's unique needs and circumstances.

How Will This Book Help You?

This book can be a helpful guide to people who want to break their gambling habit. We use a cognitive behavioural therapy (CBT) approach to guide you through practical steps and techniques that can help you towards this goal. The key idea in CBT is that how we think, feel inside, feel within our bodies, and behave are closely linked together. Changing one of these areas brings about changes in the other areas. CBT places great emphasis on our thoughts. What is going through our mind affects how we feel inside, how our body feels, and how we behave. For example, as you are reading through these lines right now, you may have thoughts about this book popping into your head. You may be thinking: 'No way can a self-help book change something as powerful as my gambling' and 'This book will be a waste of time.' Such a thought may make you feel irritated. You may even feel some tension in your body and a slight change in your breathing or your heart rate. You may experience an urge to stop reading this book and walk away. Remember: a thought can affect your emotions, body, and behaviour. Of course, the exact opposite may be happening. As you are reading these lines, the following thought may pop into your mind: 'This book sounds interesting' and 'It may be worth giving it a chance.' This could make you feel hopeful, slightly energised, and highly focused; it could motivate you to carry on reading this book and get help.

How do the above principles apply to gambling? Certain thoughts that you may not even be aware of fuel your gambling. Research has demonstrated how the random and uncontrollable nature of gambling activities compromises our rational-thinking capacity. This applies even more to those struggling with compulsive gambling. We have witnessed first-hand how our clients are affected by emotional thoughts that do not make much logical sense. After experiencing a gambling-related loss, it's not uncommon for someone gambling problematically to think: 'If I continue betting, my luck will change and I will eventually win' or 'I can't walk out without taking my money back.' These thoughts create feelings of excitement and/or apprehension, release adrenaline, pumping up the body and intensifying the urge to place another bet. Their thoughts ultimately lock them in a vicious cycle, potentially accumulating their debts and making it harder to walk away.

In contrast, someone gambling recreationally may have different thoughts after a gambling-related loss. He/she is more likely to think: 'I lost my daily limit, I am done' or 'Losing is part of gambling, never mind.' He/she is likely to feel disappointed and is perhaps despondent and low in energy but walks away anyway. The situation is the same in both scenarios: a gambling-related loss. Yet the thoughts that follow for someone gambling compulsively and someone gambling recreationally are completely different and also result in different feelings, physical sensations, and behaviours. Of course, becoming more aware of our thinking and changing it takes time. This is even more true when something as addictive as gambling has hijacked our brain and our thoughts. CBT not only aims to help you change your thinking but also focuses on all four areas – thoughts, emotions, physical sensations, behaviours – as well as other processes like your attention. In fact, in this workbook, we start by guiding you to apply some very practical ideas to restrict access to gambling and money while you are 'buying time' to build more complex skills and regain control.

CBT is an evidence-based therapy for the treatment of a gambling disorder – the official term that psychiatrists use for compulsive gambling. In other words, CBT has been tested via valid scientific methods and has been found to help a significant portion of individuals who have a gambling problem. To date, there is not a CBT model that is universally used for treating a gambling disorder. There are various CBT protocols that use numerous techniques and apply the CBT principles slightly differently. This book relies on an evidence-based approach developed by the clinical psychologist Dr Nancy Petry in the late 1990s and early 2000s in the United States. This approach heavily relies on 'cognitive restructuring' – a fancy term used to describe simple tasks such as keeping a diary, which could help you recognise and change the part of your thinking that makes you susceptible to impulsive behaviour. It also includes strategies for changing your behaviour, such as giving yourself rewards on non-gambling days and changes in your lifestyle and environment, such as avoiding places or people that could trigger your desire to gamble. Mixing cognitive and behavioural techniques together can help you achieve maximum benefit. There is also a particular focus on relapse prevention, as recovery from gambling rarely happens in a linear fashion and there will be several slips and setbacks on the way. A word of advice: don't let lapses put you off! Treat them as part of the journey rather than the end.

We have used the above CBT protocol at the National Problem Gambling Clinic in the UK, and we have also enriched the original manual with other evidence-based techniques that have been shared with hundreds of individuals over thousands of hours of clinical work undertaken in the clinic in the last ten years. We have drawn upon ideas from behavioural science about the habitual nature of gambling and state-of-the-art cognitive neuroscience research about how gambling hijacks the brain. We have also adopted notions and techniques from motivational enhancement therapy – another evidence-based therapy originally developed to help with smoking cessation, which can be used to help individuals resolve mixed feelings about dropping an addictive behaviour or other unhelpful, long-standing habits. Motivational enhancement therapy makes use of open-ended questions, invites honesty about existing concerns about the upcoming change, and encourages reflection regarding one's values and goals. It aims to remove ambivalence and make change more likely to happen. Finally, we have included techniques in metacognition and mindfulness (yes, two more fancy terms). Metacognitive techniques make you more aware of your 'thinking about your thinking', and mindfulness techniques are about living life with greater awareness and attentiveness. Okay, hopefully you are still with us after reading this last sentence! Don't worry about these 'big words' right now, as the following chapters will spell out things in simple language and use case examples.

Before reading any further, a word of warning. The philosophy of this book and our treatment programme at the National Problem Gambling Clinic is tailored towards our clients achieving total abstinence. Think of gambling like a magnet – if you are close to it, you will feel pulled towards it. You have to move quite some distance from the magnetic field not to be affected by it. If you are looking to read this book as a way of controlling your gambling, you may find it much more challenging to succeed in your goal using the techniques recommended here. In fact, later in the book, we make a clear distinction between professional, recreational, and compulsive gambling as we don't think that one can simply move from compulsive to professional or even recreational gambling. We think that individuals with a history of pathological gambling are and will be more prone to gambling-related harms as a result of a pre-existing vulnerability, via alterations in their brain, because of their previous over-reliance on gambling to manage emotions, or all of the above.

How Shall I Use This Book?

Breaking Free How To Stop Gambling guides you step by step through skills and techniques that have been found to be helpful in stopping problematic gambling and sustaining a gambling-free life. Each chapter will take you through a new set of skills and you will need courage, patience, and discipline to apply them in practice.

Some of the skills may seem easy on paper but trying to implement them in real life requires hard work. Give each set of skills your best shot before you decide if it is helpful to you.

You may need to set time aside each day to practise certain skills or make changes in your lifestyle, which you must then sustain over a period of time before you can tell how useful they are. If you move too quickly through the chapters, without giving each set of skills a fair chance, you may feel prematurely disappointed. Allow yourself enough time with each chapter. There is no point in rushing through the book before the ideas have settled. And remember, if you are reading this book to get help with a gambling problem, you may be up against a habit that has been with you for months, most likely years. How fair would it be if you only gave yourself a little time to break away from it? Trying to leave gambling behind can also be an emotional process – for many people, gambling has felt like a loyal companion and dropping this habit will entail a major change in how you live your daily life and may be accompanied by a sense of loss.

As you are going through this book, it can be useful to keep a daily record of whether you gamble or not so you can track your progress. Depending on how we feel, our memory plays tricks on us, and thus tracking will prevent you from inaccurately recalling your gambling activity or its absence. It can also be extremely rewarding for people when they look back and recognise that they have not gambled for a number of days, weeks, or months. This itself could give you the motivation to try your best to abstain on days when you have a strong desire to gamble. If you would like to record your progress, '**Tracking Your Progress**' gives you an idea of how to do this on paper or via a tracking application on your phone.

Journaling activities are a key feature of this book and you will find them in each chapter. These activities present exercises designed to help you practise important skills that can help with your recovery. Many skills found in them are meant to be practised again and again over time. Thus, you may want to make several copies of each activity so you can go back as often as you need to. You can find these activities throughout the book but they are also available to download for your personal use from the website accompanying this book.

Throughout the book, you will find many personal stories. They represent snapshots of the lives of people who, like yourself, have experienced a gambling problem. To protect privacy, these personal accounts are amalgamations of the life stories of clients that we have treated in the clinic over the years and no identifying facts or details are reported. They are used to illustrate core struggles of compulsive gambling and applications of key skills of the programme, as well as common obstacles on the road to recovery. They will hopefully help you get some perspective on your own hardships and remind you that you are not alone. Sadly, many people's lives have been negatively affected by gambling.

This workbook does not replace therapy with a qualified therapist. In fact, in a research study, Nancy Petry and her colleagues found that therapy with a trained CBT therapist alongside attendance at Gambling Anonymous (GA) meetings further improved clinical outcomes compared with a combination of a CBT workbook and GA meetings. Yet the addition of a CBT workbook to GA meetings achieved better outcomes than attendance at GA meetings alone. She also found that the more workbook exercises participants had completed, the better they did in relation to their abstinence. Thus, this book may not be a cure-all, but it can still help you make some progress; and the more effort you put into it, the greater this progress may be.

We expect that for some readers, going through the exercises of this book may be all they need for now. We would also not be surprised if some readers prefer trying self-help techniques while contemplating seeking professional help. Some readers may also live in remote locations, where access to help is not readily available, so this book may be all they can access. If you are reading this book because a loved one is affected by gambling-related harms, you may be looking for a better under-standing of their problem gambling and what changes are required so you can help them break away from it.

No matter your reason for reading this book, if by the end of it you feel that you need to seek further professional help with a qualified therapist, that is absolutely fine. In fact, we would be very pleased to know that we have helped you take the decision to seek further help. We also expect that some people may wish to use this book alongside their therapy. We don't see a problem with this. In fact, it's a common practice in CBT for therapists to recommend self-help books alongside sessions and to sometimes use these books to structure their therapy.

Tracking Your Progress

It can be useful to make a daily record of whether you gamble or not. There are several aims of this task as described below.

Available Tracking Apps

Recoverme (Free for a Year; Apple and Android)

Recoverme is a mobile health app designed to help those who suffer from a gambling addiction. The app uses CBT and mindfulness techniques to help you recover from gambling-related harms. Some of the techniques employed by the app are also described in this book. The app also has a diary feature. This will help you improve your self-awareness and allow you to monitor your progress through this journey.

Nomo (Free; Apple and Android)

Nomo is an abstinence counter app which allows you to track how long you've gone without gambling as well as how much time and money you've saved. When you reach particular milestones without gambling, achievements will be unlocked. A daily journal can also be used to log what emotions or thoughts you are experiencing each day.

The 'accountability partners' function allows users to match with other people trying to abstain from gambling for mutual support. If you feel the urge to gamble, you can reach out to these partners for help. The app also has a number of short exercises designed to help you refocus when you feel the urge to gamble.

I Am Sober (Free; Apple and Android)

I Am Sober is an abstinence counter app which allows you to track how long you've gone without gambling. You can track how much money or time you've saved by not gambling and unlock achievements based on how long you've abstained for.

Each day you can log whether or not you've gambled, keep track of how you found that day (easy, hard, impossible, etc.), and log what you did and thought that day. The app also allows you to see what particular activities are linked to difficult days, so you know to try and avoid them in the future. Daily motivational quotes can help you focus on taking each day as it comes.

Way of Life (Free; Apple and Android)

Way of Life is a habit-building app which allows you to track days where you do and don't gamble. You can also add notes to individual days to keep a record of how you felt that day or what triggered urges to gamble. You can set reminders each day to update the in-app journal.

Over time, you will be able to build up a week-by-week trend, seeing what periods you managed to avoid gambling as well as keeping track of which weeks have been good weeks and which weeks have been challenging. You can then try and make links between how difficult you found that week and what activities you were doing.

Quitzilla (Free; Android Only)

Quitzilla is an abstinence counter app which allows you to keep track of how long you have avoided gambling. You can see how close you are to your next milestone as well as how much money and time you've saved by avoiding gambling. It provides a quote of the day, which can help you to focus on avoiding gambling.

Tracking on Paper

If you are unable to download a tracking app, or would prefer to avoid using a smartphone, you can also keep track of whether you gamble or not on paper, using a tracking graph. In the graph, each horizontal block represents one day. In each block, you are to represent whether you gamble or not by drawing a diagonal line or a horizontal line.

Draw a *diagonal* line going upward for each day that you do not gamble – like this /. If you have a lapse and do gamble, draw a *horizontal* line for that day, like this ___. Once you stop gambling, go back to drawing diagonal lines again, going upward towards the right-hand top corner of the page. An example is shown below, starting on the 21st of the month.

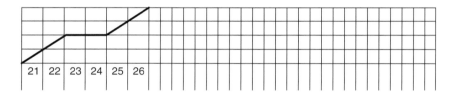

In the example above, this person did not gamble on the 21st or 22nd, then had a slip that lasted two days, represented by the straight lines, and then went back to not gambling on the 25th and 26th. The graph would continue like this throughout the month.

Your task is to get as far up to the top of the page as you can, with each small step indicating days of non-gambling. The graph will cover a time period of about a month. This graph will help you see how much progress you have made.

Keep the tracking graph somewhere handy at home and complete it daily.

Marking My Progress

Month

Starting at the bottom left-hand corner, the idea is that you will draw a diagonal line going upward for each day you don't gamble on this chart (like this /). If you ever have a lapse and gamble, draw a horizontal line for each gambling day, like this ___. Once you stop gambling, revert to drawing diagonal lines again, going upward towards the right-hand top corner of the page.

Marking My Progress Chart

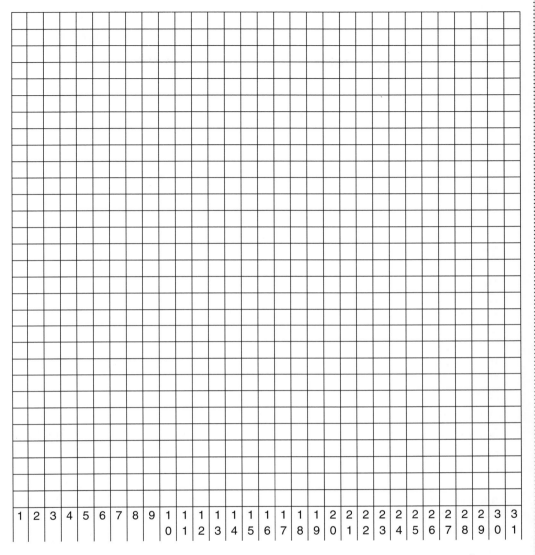

| 1 | 2 | 3 | 4 | 5 | 6 | 7 | 8 | 9 | 10 | 11 | 12 | 13 | 14 | 15 | 16 | 17 | 18 | 19 | 20 | 21 | 22 | 23 | 24 | 25 | 26 | 27 | 28 | 29 | 30 | 31 |

Write the start date at the bottom left-hand corner and each square represents a new day.

Adapted from: Petry, N. (2004). Pathological gambling: Etiology, comorbidity and treatment. Washington: American Psychological Association

2   How Do I Know if I Have a Gambling Disorder?

Andre Geel

If you are reading this book, the chances are that you or someone you know has a gambling disorder or is affected by harms related to gambling. In this chapter, we will look at what a gambling disorder looks like and what you can do about identifying it. Finding out whether gambling is in fact problematic is the first stage before action to overcome it.

The Honeymoon Period

Most people have gambled in one way or another in their lives and most of them have found this to be fun, enjoyable, and not problematic. This behaviour has been recreational and a pastime that in many cases people have not even thought about as being a problem.

In fact, a gambling disorder doesn't start out as a problem at all but rather an enjoyable behaviour. This is the honeymoon period, which quickly turns into misery.

It's when that enjoyable behaviour becomes persistent, repetitive, and expensive that it begins to look more like a problem or an addiction. At that point it begins to affect your relationships, finances, work, and other parts of your life in very negative ways.

It is often the case that other people see you developing your problem before you realise yourself. It might be that it affects those closest to you but you have not noticed it yet or you don't want to admit it. Often in the early stages, you don't see yourself as having a problem at all and are puzzled by how others might be worried for you. This can persist for some time and it might take some extreme situations to highlight it as a problem.

How Can I Tell that It's a Problem?

You may now be wondering what it takes to tell if you have a gambling problem, especially since being oblivious can be common in the early stages.

❖ Firstly, have you ever lied about your gambling to anyone, have you ever tried to conceal the fact that you've gambled and have you been deceitful about the fact that you gamble?

One of the simplest ways of seeing if you have a gambling problem is to check in with yourself and ask if you have tried to conceal or minimise your gambling. If you have, then there is a very good chance that even you feel there is something wrong about your gambling. This is called the LIE/BET method and it's probably the simplest way to begin to look at whether you have a gambling disorder.

❖ Secondly, have you ever bet more than you can afford to lose?

People for whom gambling is a problem tend to 'chase their losses' by betting increasingly larger amounts of money than they can afford to spend on gambling. On the other hand, those people who gamble in a recreational fashion only play with as much money as they can afford to lose and are not trying to win at any cost.

If you answered yes to either or both of these questions, then there is a good chance that gambling is possibly problematic for you and you need to look further into it, so keep reading.

To examine this further, there are a number of brief assessments or tests that can be used to establish more specifically if you have a problem or not. One of the most reliable and simplest of these is the Problem Gambling Severity Index (PGSI) – one of the tools we use in our clinic. It only has a few questions and a very simple scoring system which will allow you to assess the nature of your problem. This is presented in **the 'Problem Gambling Severity Index'.**

The 'Official' Criteria

Your score on the Problem Gambling Severity Index (PGSI) may help you realise whether you are at risk of suffering any harms as a result of gambling. However, it does not entirely allow you to appreciate the full extent of the negative impact that gambling has on your life.

The 'official' view on what constitutes a gambling problem is found in the *Diagnostic and Statistical Manual of Mental Disorders 5* (DSM5), which is something like the bible for psychiatrists in the American Psychiatric Association and across the world. You can find their criteria in '**The "Official" Criteria of a Gambling Disorder'.** Going through them may well help you appreciate further if you have a gambling problem and to what extent.

Problem Gambling Severity Index

To assess further if your gambling is problematic, complete the following questionnaire by answering the nine questions and scoring them accordingly.

Problem Gambling Severity Index

The Problem Gambling Severity Index (PGSI) is the standardised measure of at-risk behaviour in gambling. It is a tool based on research on the common signs and consequences of problematic gambling. Assessing where you are now can help you make an informed decision on how to go forward.

How Does It Work?
The PGSI quiz asks you to self-assess your gambling behaviour over the past 12 months by scoring yourself against nine questions.

Answer the quiz questions below in reference to your gambling behaviour over the past 12 months and then score them according to the key underneath.

1. Have you bet more than you could really afford to lose?	0 Never	1 Sometimes	2 Often	3 Always
2. Have you needed to gamble with larger amounts of money to get the same feeling of excitement?	0 Never	1 Sometimes	2 Often	3 Always
3. Have you gone back on another day to try to win back the money you lost?	0 Never	1 Sometimes	2 Often	3 Always
4. Have you borrowed money or sold anything to gamble?	0 Never	1 Sometimes	2 Often	3 Always
5. Have you felt that you might have a problem with gambling?	0 Never	1 Sometimes	2 Often	3 Always
6. Have people criticised your betting or told you that you had a gambling problem, whether or not you thought it was true?	0 Never	1 Sometimes	2 Often	3 Always
7. Have you felt guilty about the way you gamble or what happens when you gamble?	0 Never	1 Sometimes	2 Often	3 Always

8. Has gambling caused you any health problems, including stress or anxiety?	0 Never	1 Sometimes	2 Often	3 Always
9. Has your gambling caused any financial problems for you or your household?	0 Never	1 Sometimes	2 Often	3 Always

Key: Never: (score 0); Sometimes: (score 1); Often/most of the time: (score 2); Always: (score 3).

Add up the scores for the nine questions above using the key and that total will indicate which category your score falls in.

What is your total score? _____

The score will tell you whether you fall into one of four categories – non-problem gambling, low risk gambling, moderate risk gambling, or problem gambling – and whether a further, more detailed assessment might help you understand the problem better as well as seeking the appropriate treatment.

Adapted from: Ferris, J., & Wynne, H. (2001). The Canadian problem gambling index: Final report. Ottawa: Canadian Centre on Substance Abuse

What Do the Categories Mean?

Non-problem Gambling: Score 0

- Gambling with no negative consequences and closest to what we would call recreational gambling.

Low-risk Gambling: Score 1–2

- A person in the low-risk gambling category experiences a low level of problems with few or no identified negative consequences. For example, they may very occasionally spend over the limit or feel somewhat guilty about their gambling.

Moderate-risk Gambling: Score 3–7

- Someone in the moderate-risk category experiences a moderate level of problems leading to some negative consequences. For example, they may sometimes spend more than they can afford, lose track of time, or feel guilty about their gambling.

Problem Gambling: Score 8 or Above

- In this category, a person gambles with negative consequences and a possible loss of control. For example, they may often spend over the limit, gamble to win back money and feel stressed about their gambling.

It is likely that if you fall into the last two categories that your gambling has become problematic, and that seeking help would be advisable and useful. The rest of this manual is designed to help you in this regard and assist you as part of a comprehensive treatment package.

The 'Official' Criteria of a Gambling Disorder

The official definition of a gambling disorder entails nine distinct behaviours. You will need to mark at least four of them as relevant to you in the last 12 months to have a formal diagnosis.

* You need to gamble more and more money in order to achieve the level of excitement you are seeking.
* You are restless or irritable when attempting to cut down or stop your gambling.
* You have made repeated and unsuccessful efforts to control, cut back, or stop your gambling.
* You are often preoccupied with gambling, such as having persistent thoughts of past gambling experiences, planning your next venture, and thinking of ways to get more money with which to gamble.
* You often gamble when you feel distressed, helpless, guilty, anxious, or depressed.
* After losing money gambling, you often return another day to 'get even' and try to win your money back. This is called 'chasing' losses.
* You have lied to conceal the extent of your gambling.
* You have jeopardised or lost significant relationships, jobs, or educational or career opportunities because of your gambling.
* You have relied on others to provide money to relieve your financial situation caused by gambling.

The more of these behaviours you engage in, the greater your gambling disorder may be.

Recreational and Professional Gambling

Another way to help you further appreciate how much of a problem your gambling is is to contrast problem and compulsive gambling with recreational and professional gambling.

We mentioned as part of the paragraphs above that non-problem gambling might be also termed *recreational* gambling. This is when a person gambles for fun and does not mind losing the money that they gamble. They see gambling as a pastime and not as a means of winning money, and in many cases would see the money as well spent after an evening or days' gambling. Recreational gamblers would often also only gamble on certain special occasions such as horseraces, special sporting events, and holidays.

The next type of gambling is *professional* gambling – often portrayed erroneously in films as the suave secret agent who never loses a bet, which glamourises gambling. In actual fact, professional gamblers tend to be very careful and cautious individuals who are using the various forms of gambling in order to support a steady income. Professional gamblers will not bet ('invest') more than they are prepared to lose and tend to estimate their odds and returns in a very pragmatic fashion. They will tend to bet with a fixed amount of money over a fixed period of time and not exceed these limits. They will have calculated the returns and often look at long-term rewards rather than short-term wins.

Thus, professional gambling may look more boring and less prestigious than one may have originally thought!

If you gamble problematically it is likely that you have gone through times when you would see your gambling as an innocent hobby (recreational) or as a way of making money (professional). However, both types of gambling are distinctly different from *compulsive* and problematic gambling. Recreational and professional gambling do not come with a bunch of negative effects. You may be hoping that your gambling will make you rich or offer a nice break from your worries, but the reality is that a gambling problem will most probably bring debts and make you chase your losses in an attempt to make back money. In fact, if you gamble compulsively, you very seldom stick to the limits that you set on the amount of money you are betting.

Recreational, professional, and compulsive gambling are not entirely distinct. Some people can move from one to the other without even realising. However, when gambling becomes a problem, it's very difficult to revert back to recreational or professional gambling.

John's story is a good example of how this can happen.

John's Story

John was an aspiring accountant who took up playing poker as a hobby while studying at university. It was a way of taking time out from his busy and intense schedule to spend some time with like-minded friends in an engaging and mentally stimulating activity. Not much money was wagered and it was really just to add to the excitement of the game itself. There was little interest in how much money was won in the end, it was rather the enjoyment of playing the game and the skill involved.

By his second year, John had developed quite a reputation as a skilful poker player and was consistently winning. In fact, his winning was so consistent he had been able to buy himself a new laptop and pay off one of his courses that year.

He didn't think much about his hobby and whether it was gambling or not, and indeed the fun he had reminded him of his experiences as a child when he used to place bets on the Grand National – and other lesser races – for his grandfather when the family went for weekend lunches at the local pub. It gave him a sense of pride at being able to engage with the adults in such a grown-up event.

He often found those happy memories coming back to him more and more as he played on into the early hours of the morning at the poker table.

At the start of his third year, John had decided that he would be able to buy a car and pay off much of his university debts if he was able to win enough in this coming year. He calculated that he would need about £20,000 to cover his expenses.

During that third year he noticed how much more difficult the course seemed and also that he was spending increasing amounts of time at the poker table and staying on later into the evenings. His concentration regarding his studies was not as good as it used to be and he was focusing more intently on each poker game and how much he was winning or losing.

He had bought his car on hire purchase and noticed that he wasn't winning quite enough to pay back the instalments, so he used part of his student loan to place bigger and more frequent bets on his poker games. He noticed that he had less motivation to attend his lectures recently and also that he did not feel the same enjoyment playing poker but was rather more interested in whether he was winning or losing. He was no longer playing for the fun of it but rather to try and recoup some of the losses that he had recently been making. He was sure he would win it all back by the end of the year.

By the end of the year John was £10,000 in debt and had used his student loan to pay off his gambling debts. His car had been repossessed and his parents had stepped in to help him continue with his studies. They had noticed a change in his attitude towards university at the beginning of his third year and that he had lost some interest in the courses that he originally found stimulating and engaging. At that time John did not think it was a problem and thought his parents were over-concerned at his interest in poker. To him, it was still recreational and just a bit of fun.

It was at the end of that third year that John finally came around to appreciate his parents' concern for his behaviour and realised that he now found himself in a very problematic situation. He had not seen the gradual deterioration in his interest in his university studies and his growing preoccupation with his gambling activity. Nor had he noticed his lack of concern as his mounting losses and the value of the money he was gambling.

All of that became apparent at the end of his third and final year once he had weighed up the pros and cons of his behaviour over the preceding three years. It was at that point after a long conversation with his parents that he decided to take the first steps in his recovery, contacted his GP, and found a link to a gambling helpline that was able to direct him to a gambling treatment centre.

Forms of Gambling: Choice and Skills

Even after reading the above sections, you may still remain unsure whether your gambling is problematic. This could be because you think that there is something different about your preferred form of gambling that does not classify it as gambling!

Everyone has gambled in one way or another – it can be argued – from playing the stock market to a 'flutter on the horses', buying a lottery ticket or tombola at the local fair.

These days, with the Internet, you can gamble anywhere, at any time, on any device, in addition to the more traditional places such as casinos, betting shops, racecourses, pubs, bars, and corner shops for scratch cards and lottery tickets.

These wide and varied options of gambling fall into different types. Firstly: chance-based gambling – such as playing the lottery, scratch-card roulette, bingo, or gaming machines. In these instances, the results are random and cannot be influenced by the player. Secondly: skill-based gambling – such as betting on races, playing poker or blackjack, shares in the stock market, spread betting, or cryptocurrency. In these instances, your ability, skill, or knowledge can influence whether you win or lose.

Take a Minute to Think

- Are there any types of gambling that you do not view as gambling?

- Why not?

If your preferred way of gambling is chance-based, then the person playing the game has the belief that there is some formula behind the system of winning. You believe that if you pull the lever in a certain way, or for a certain number of times, or wait a certain period of time, that the machine will pay out. You might believe there are certain lucky machines, or that luck or other factors might influence the outcome of the win. This belief system is often what keeps you gambling for longer and what maintains a problematic gambling behaviour. In Chapter 10, we discuss how this could be a form of illogical thinking, called a mental trap.

In the case of skill-based gambling, you often believe that you have particular skills that allow you to win a specific game, and often over-estimate these skills as the game progresses. You may also overestimate the amount of influence you have over the game, not realising that there is an element of chance as well. Again, this belief system that you have a particular skill often keeps you in the game for longer than is safe or sensible and results in losses mounting.

If, by now, you are still unsure about whether gambling does more harm than good for you, noticing the reactions of important others in your life or reading the next chapter on motivation may help you further decide.

Significant Others Can Be the First to Notice that There Is a Problem

Family members, friends, or significant others will often be the first people to notice this behaviour and its negative consequences. They will notice you spending more and more time gambling and being less and less interested in the amount of money that you might be losing. They might notice that you become preoccupied with professing a 'formula' for winning – on the horses, in the casino, at blackjack, or on the stock market. They might also notice that you have lost interest in things that you normally find enjoyable, such as recreation, hobbies, sport, and other things. You have less time for people close to you and might appear more agitated and distressed, particularly in relation to your gambling activity.

You might have noticed that family members or people close to you have commented on your gambling behaviour recently or in the past before you thought that you had a problem. It is often the case that people close to you might notice your behaviour change before you do and might show concerns before you yourself are concerned. At this point, it is useful to take note of this, as this might be the early signs of a gambling problem. If you have a supportive family, partner, or friend, it might be possible to speak to them about what they have noticed, and this might be the start of helping manage this problem.

If you have borrowed money to gamble, hidden your debts, have jeopardised your situation at work, have become preoccupied and distressed with gambling – these are things that family members and others often notice earlier on and become concerned about – possibly long before you realise that you have a problem. If this is the case, it is good to explore this further with trusted family and friends, to see if this applies to you and to see what solutions might be found to overcome it.

Take a Minute to Think

- Approach someone who cares about you and ask them to tell you if they are genuinely worried about your gambling. What have they noticed? What do they worry about?

What's Next?

So far we've looked at how to identify the problem. The next chapter is what can be done about it. Gambling disorder is a relatively new disorder, but interestingly enough there has been extensive research into its treatment in a relatively short time and the results are very promising. The best and most effective treatment is cognitive behavioural therapy – upon which most of this manual is based. It is an evidence-based psychological intervention that is designed to turn around this problem behaviour and get you back on the route to a healthier lifestyle. It looks at your thoughts and your behaviour and how the two interact and influence one another. How thinking influences your behaviour, and how, by changing what you think about, can result in you acting differently. It might not be as difficult as you think to change your mind and behaviour!

Whatever the extent of your gambling-related harms by following this manual's programme, there is every chance that you can improve and even overcome the worst of it. Gambling disorder is treatable, and the evidence suggests that there are good chances of recovery, and this has been the experience of our clinic and the outcomes that have been achieved.

This manual gives you access to some of those interventions in an accessible and practical format. Many of them will be effective and practical in their own right but please remember there's no substitute for consulting a qualified psychologist or practitioner in the field in order to ensure that they are applied in a correct and effective manner.

Skills Practice

- Complete the PGSI – Problem Gambling Severity Index scale – and note the score and where you fall within the categories.

- If it is within the problem field, then you may want to check how many of the 'official' criteria are relevant to you in order to assess the extent of the problem.

- Draw the line between the recreational/professional aspects of gambling and when it becomes a problem.

- Recognise all types of gambling for what they are – including chance and skill-based gambling.

Takeaway Points for Affected Significant Others

- Individuals presenting with a gambling problem – particularly for the first time – need to recognise and acknowledge that this behaviour is a problem before they take action to change it.

- Often you, as an important person in their lives, see it first, before they have realised it themselves. This may feel difficult for you, but being able to pick up early signs may be a great help.

- The questionnaire and the formal criteria presented here are a good start to help the person appreciate the nature and extent of their problem.

3 'I Should Quit but I Don't Want To': Increasing Motivation

Dolors Manuel-Riu

Our levels of motivation hardly ever stay the same. Some days, we may have a very strong desire to change a habit and then the following day we may feel far less determined. Other times, we may not view a habit as a problem but feel persuaded or coaxed into making certain changes by someone close to us. Can you think of an example of a specific behaviour that you or a friend felt like changing but had mixed feelings about? It could be something ordinary, such as exercising, having a healthy diet or going to bed early. Perhaps you were persuaded by someone else to try this and despite initial enthusiasm, there were times when it felt difficult to persevere.

The same is the case when challenging gambling habits. If you are reading this workbook, it is likely that you are considering some changes. Part of you may be thinking you should stop gambling because it is causing some problems and distress in your life. However, another part of you may still enjoy it and feel attracted or compelled to gamble.

Matt's Story

Matt thinks that his gambling is getting out of control. He is spending more money than he can afford and has started borrowing from his family and using his credit card to pay his debts. His gambling has started affecting his family life. He finds himself lying to his partner, giving excuses and spending less time at home with their children. His partner has told him that he needs to stop. Gambling is affecting Matt's mood and he is stressed and constantly worried about his debts. Matt has problems sleeping, which has started affecting his performance at work. He knows that gambling is causing problems, yet he continues to gamble as he believes that with a good win, he could pay his debt and solve his difficulties.

When you think about making changes to your gambling habits, it's worth considering the whole picture. It is important to consider why you are trying to stop or control gambling and also to reflect on what compels you to gamble in the first place. If your desire to change comes from trying to please someone else, such as your partner, parent, employer, or anyone else who has asked you to adjust your gambling, you may find it harder to stay motivated. Instead, you are far more likely to succeed in making changes if the desire for change comes from within you.

The Different Sides of Gambling: A Decisional Balance

This chapter will help you to make a decision about your gambling. The first exercise is called a decisional balance and it is a good way of weighing up the pros and cons of a particular behaviour. Assessing the pros and cons of both stopping and not stopping gambling is a way to fully consider all the reasons for a possible change.

Pros and Cons of Change

Let's start by looking at gambling from all sides. Take some time to think and answer the four questions below. Write down all the reasons you can think of in each of the four boxes of the decisional balance exercise. Try to be as open and honest with yourself as possible.

To help you with this exercise, we present Matt's decisional balance as an example.

1. What Do I Like about Gambling?

Sometimes people can find it hard to remember what the positives of gambling are or were. You may need to think back to when you were last gambling, or it may be surprisingly fresh in your mind what is good about gambling. Either way, pause and think:

> *What's good about gambling? What do you like? How does it make you feel? What are the feelings after a win? What is the purpose of the gambling for you? How does it meet your needs?*

2. What Do I Dislike about Gambling?

Often people find this part easier. However, you need to think broadly about all of the consequences of gambling. Think about mental and physical health, work, legal consequences, finances, and relationships.

> *What are the negative impacts of your gambling? How is it affecting your life? How is it affecting the lives of your loved ones? What has gambling prevented you from doing or achieving in your life? Where might you be now if you had never gambled?*

3. What Do I Dislike about Not Gambling?

Gambling serves a function for you and when gambling stops there is likely to be something of a gap. It is important to know what will be difficult for you when you stop gambling as these needs, if ignored, could put you at risk of lapsing.

> *What is hard for you when you do not gamble? What do you fear if you stop gambling? What is missing in your life when you do not gamble?*

What Do I Like about Not Gambling?

This is not just the absence of negative things. You need to visualise a world without gambling. Imagine that a global ban on gambling is put in place tomorrow and gambling disappears completely.

> *What will that world be like for you? How would your life be different? What will change in your life? What will you be able to do? How would your family life or relationships be?*

Matt's decisional balance

What I like about gambling/Pros	What I dislike about gambling/Cons
• The excitement • The possibility of winning money • Blocks the stress about my debt and relationship difficulties with my partner	• Losing money • Growing debt • Lying to my partner • Problems with my partner and family • Makes me feel very stressed and anxious • Difficulties sleeping • It's affecting me at work, and I worry that they may lay me off • Makes feel down and depressed • I feel consumed by it

What I dislike about NOT gambling	What I like about NOT gambling
• I would have to face reality and pay my debt • I would not be able to escape • I worry that I may not be able to cope with the urges to gamble	• I would have money • I would have no debt • I would feel better about myself • My relationship with my partner and family would be better • I would have peace of mind • I would be able to do and enjoy things I like • I would be able to move forward and have a future

My decisional balance

What I like about gambling/Pros	What I dislike about gambling/Cons

What I dislike about NOT gambling	What I like about NOT gambling

Take a Minute to Think

You may wonder how a simple exercise, like writing down the pros and cons of gambling, can help you change a habit that may have followed you for many years. Let's have a look:

1. It slows you down and helps you to decide wisely.
2. It enables you to see the bigger picture, including conflicting aspects.
3. It helps you decide what action to take and how ready you are to do so.
4. It acts as a memory aid.

Decide Wisely

Decisional balances can be used for all sorts of decisions; we tend to weigh up the pros and cons of behaviours throughout the day. Think about crossing the road: it would be quicker and easier to just walk out into the road without having to look for cars or wait for a gap to appear. Yet, you don't do it. Why not? This is because the negative consequences and the possible risk of being seriously injured outweigh the convenience of crossing the road without thinking.

In your head, you compute a quick decisional balance about the pros and cons of stepping into the road multiple times per day. However, most likely, you are not aware of the thinking process that has gone on in your head every time you cross the road. This is because your thinking is automatic and subconscious in situations that are very familiar. At some point in the past, you would have had to learn how to cross the road, and this would have been a more conscious and deliberate process. Most decisions have to be made consciously until they become habitual over time.

The use of the decisional balance exercise aims to help with the same process; your gambling habits have become automatic and to change this you need to be more conscious about the positives and negatives of your decision to gamble. Thus, the helpful thing about this exercise is that it can slow you down and make you weigh up the different aspects to gambling. This can help you make a wise decision about your gambling habits rather than acting impulsively.

Now look back at the top two boxes of your decisional balance and reflect on the pros and cons of gambling. What do you see?

Take a Minute to Think

- How important are the things in the 'pros' column compared to the 'cons'?

  _____
  _____
  _____
  _____
  _____

- Is there a theme about short lived versus long term impacts?

  _____
  _____
  _____
  _____
  _____

- Are there any opposites?

  _____
  _____
  _____
  _____
  _____

- What worries you most about your gambling?

  _____
  _____
  _____
  _____
  _____

> • What makes you think you need to change your gambling?
>
> _____
>
> _____
>
> _____
>
> _____
>
> _____

Holding the Big Picture in Mind

Our minds tend to think one way or another about things; holding two competing thoughts in our minds at the same time requires more effort. You may find that you are aware of positive thoughts about gambling just before gambling and remember all the negative thoughts afterwards. The decisional balance is a tool that allows you to see both sides before you act.

Take a look again at the two top boxes of your completed decisional balance sheet once again.

What I like about gambling/Pros	What I dislike about gambling/Cons

Now in your mind remove the line that separates the top two boxes; this is what gambling means for you. In Matt's example it looks like this:

My gambling: What I like and don't like	
Excitement	Anxiety
Money	Debt
Winning	Losing
Escape from problems	Stress
	Depression
	Sleep difficulties
	Lies

Your brain is set up to think either positively or negatively about gambling, usually positively before gambling and negatively afterwards. Your job is to retrain your mind to think about gambling in an **AND** fashion. The reality is that gambling will have positives but also negatives, a **YES, BUT …**

So, back to the decisional balance exercise: the top two boxes represent all of gambling for you. As much as the outcomes in the left-hand box are true, equally so are the outcomes in the right-hand box. If Gambling for you has become problematic, it will bring all of the things listed on the negative side of your balance sheet, so if you decide to continue with it, you must acknowledge it all.

Goal Setting and Readiness

As you now start seeing both sides of gambling, you are ready for the next step: to decide where you want to go next with your gambling and how ready you are to take this step.

The '**My Goals and How Ready I Am to Pursue Them**' exercise helps you decide upon the direction you want to head to. Do you want to continue to gamble? Do you want to quit gambling? Do you want to find a way to reduce it? Bear in mind that if gambling has become problematic, giving it up completely may be a more appropriate route than trying to control it. However, the final call is yours. Regardless of what you decide, this exercise is about setting a goal and committing to it. Some of the questions in the worksheet also prompt you to consider how ready you are to carry out these changes.

Using Decisional Balance as a Memory Aid

As further explained in Chapter 10, where we look at certain thinking traps, gambling plays a trick on your memory. You remember more clearly gambling wins than losses. Our minds are generally better able to minimise losses and to forget them. Remembering all of the losses in our life would make us feel depressed. In fact, this is what happens in depression; people demonstrate a thinking bias towards negative memories. When it comes to gambling, however, you know only too well that the larger picture for you is one of overall loss. The trouble is that it is hard to remember this when you feel the urge to gamble. This is why having a memory aid is so useful.

At times when it is difficult to access the rational part of your brain, a cue card can be used as a strategy to remind you of the problems that gambling has caused you. Examples of such times are when you experience cravings or when you remember past wins. '**Creating Your Personal Cue Card**' guides you through how to create your own cue card, drawing on the decisional balance exercise.

To help you with the '**My Goals and How Ready I Am to Pursue Them**' exercise, you may want to have a look at what Matt's plan of change would look like, in the following box.

Matt's Plan of Change

My goal is to stop gambling completely. This week I will exclude myself from my local bookmakers and I will ask my partner to help me manage my money.

How important is it for me to stop gambling right now? 10

What makes it that important? It's affecting my mental health, it's destroying my life, and I will lose my wife and children.

How confident am I right now about stopping gambling? 5

What gives me that confidence? I stopped for a few months two years ago when I sought help.

What can I do to increase my confidence? Having someone that helps me go through it and having the support of my partner.

What are my first steps to achieving my goal?

This week I will talk to my partner and ask her to help manage my money.

I will exclude myself from the local bookmakers.

My Goals and How Ready I Am to Pursue Them

Having considered both the positive and negative sides to gambling, what would you like to do now?

Are you ready to make a decision? If so, what is your goal and what is it that you want to achieve? Change is much easier if you have a clear goal in mind.

My goal is _____
_____
_____

How important is it for me to stop gambling right now? (From 1 to 10) _____
_____
_____

What makes it that important? _____

Is stopping gambling important enough for me to make the change?

If it is not important at all then maybe it is not the right time for me to stop gambling.

If its importance is between 5 and 10 think: What would make stopping gambling more important?

How confident am I right now about stopping gambling? (From 1 to 10) _____
_____
_____

What gives me that confidence? _____
_____
_____
_____
_____
_____

Take a look at your scores, for example, if you have a 3, what is it that made you write a 3 instead of a 1? What is it that makes you feel confident?

Also, think what might need to happen for your confidence to move up a point, say from a 3 to a 4? What could you do right now to make your confidence move up even slightly? Is there anything that was useful in the past when you tried to change or quit another habit? How would you know that things are changing?

Is there anything I can do to improve my confidence? _____
_____
_____
_____

What are my first steps to achieving my goal? _____
_____
_____
_____

Creating Your Personal Cue Card

Reading your personal cue card will help you to recall the negatives of gambling and the positives of not gambling. Using a cue card or a piece of paper, list the main three things that will happen if you continue to gamble and the main three things that will happen if you stop gambling. They have to be meaningful personal statements, things that really matter to you. The cue card will act as a reminder of your conviction to stop gambling. You can keep it in paper form, electronically, or take a picture of it.

Matt's Cue Card

If I gamble _____

- I will lose my partner and children
- My debt will never stop
- I will lose my job

If I stop gambling _____

- I will have money to do things I like
- I will be less stressed and feel better about myself
- My children will have a better life

My Cue Card

If I gamble _____

- _____
- _____
- _____

If I stop gambling _____

- _____
- _____
- _____

Skills Practice

- Complete your decisional balance to see the overall impact of gambling in your life.

- Write your aims in relation to gambling and the first steps you wish to take.

- Use your cue card to remember the reasons why you want to stop gambling, especially when you have a craving.

Takeaway Points for Affected Significant Others

- Remember that fluctuations in motivation are normal and affect all of us.

- Individuals affected by a gambling problem may have mixed conflicting feelings about stopping gambling.

- Do not push or coax people into change as it will have the opposite effect.

- Help increase someone's motivation by helping them see the negatives of gambling and the positives of stopping.

- Support them in their decision to stop gambling and with their plan of change.

4 'Buying Time': Limiting Access to Money and Gambling

Zoe Delaney

This chapter is about *reducing your opportunities to gamble* by limiting your access to money and gambling itself. By limiting your access, you are buying yourself time, which you can then use to apply the skills described in the following chapters of this book.

Stimulus Control

Before psychiatrists officially recognised gambling disorder as an addictive behaviour, they had classified it as an impulse control disorder. This was because people could often find themselves gambling without making a conscious decision to do so. Once exposed to something that reminds them about gambling (a gambling stimulus), they may gamble automatically, with little to no awareness.

Gambling stimuli are anything that make you think about gambling. It can be a thought, feeling, individual, or object. Anything from pay day, to walking past the bookmakers, or seeing an advert, can make you think about gambling. Difficult emotions, such as anxiety or low mood, or positive emotions, such as excitement, can also be gambling stimuli.

When exposed to a gambling stimulus you will likely experience physical symptoms within your body, such as an increased heart rate or restlessness. These symptoms, often described as cravings, can lead you to gamble as an automatic or impulsive reaction. Our brains have developed this process as a way of making connections and creating shortcuts; you will read more about this in the following two chapters.

A Russian scientist, Pavlov, developed a theory by experimenting with dogs that helps explain this process. Unlike other dog training, in Pavlov's experiments with dogs, someone would ring a bell any time the dogs were fed, causing them to salivate. Over time, the dogs would salivate every time they heard the bell, even if food was not present. They learned to associate the bell with food and this produced a physical response.

The same thing happens with gambling. Over time your brain links gambling stimuli with gambling itself. Eventually, the stimuli produce a physical response or 'craving', encouraging you to gamble. You will hear more about how to cope with cravings in Chapter 7, but one of the first steps you can take is to introduce stimulus control strategies.

It is important to limit yourself to gambling stimuli when you first decide to stop gambling, to reduce the chances of you experiencing cravings that you may act on.

However, this can be difficult, as you do not always have control over your environment or the gambling stimuli present. Stimulus control strategies allow you to create space between the stimuli and gambling so you have time to think and act.

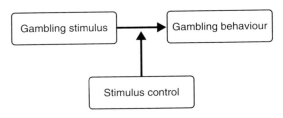

Stimulus Control Strategies

Stimulus control strategies help by blocking the impulsive nature of gambling. They allow you to have a **second thought** and consider whether gambling is something you want to do.

Take a Minute to Think

Imagine a fire triangle. You need three components to be able to have a fire, they are heat, fuel, and oxygen. If you remove one of these components, the fire is unable to start.

This is the same for gambling. Three components are needed to 'fuel' gambling, they are gambling thoughts, access to money, and access to gambling. If you remove one of these components, you are unable to gamble.

But … it is hard to not think about gambling when you are first trying to stop. This is why we do not cover gambling thoughts and how to deal with them until Chapter 10. Initially, it is easier to remove or reduce your access to money or gambling itself.

Reduce Access to Money

There are several ways you can reduce your access to money and limit your opportunities to gamble. Below are lists of strategies you can use to reduce your access through changing how you manage your cash, bank cards, and bank accounts.

This list is based on feedback we've received from individuals treated at the National Problem Gambling Clinic based on what they have found useful.

Cash

- Only carry the exact amount of money you need for the day, e.g. £10 for lunch and travel.
- Do not carry spare money for 'emergencies' as these rarely happen.
- Accept that you would be happy to lose the money you have in your pocket.
- Purchase vouchers for services you use regularly, e.g. your local supermarket.

Bank Cards

- Leave bank cards at home or give them to someone to look after.
- Order a new bank card and ask someone you trust to remove the three-digit security code on the back of the card, so you cannot use it online.

Bank Accounts

- Hand over control of your bank account to your someone you trust.
- Set a withdrawal limit on your bank account.
- Transfer spare money to a limited access savings account.
- Get your salary or benefits paid into someone else's account and have them transfer you small amounts of money.
- Request another person gets alerts if you spend over a specified amount.
- Join a bank that allows you to block gambling transactions on your account. In the UK, such accounts are Monzo, Starling, Barclays, or Lloyds.

Reduce Access to Gambling

Another strategy you can use to limit the opportunity to gamble is to reduce your access to gambling itself by signing up to self-exclusion schemes. Once signed up, gambling companies must close your accounts and no longer allow you to gamble on their premises or websites. The duration of the self-exclusion depends on the service provider so it is important you are aware what each service offers.

Below are a number of self-exclusion services that operate within the UK. For services in your local area, contact your local gambling support service or speak to staff at the gambling premises you visit.

We recommend that you put as many strategies as possible in place, even for forms of gambling that you do not currently use, to limit your opportunities to gamble as much as possible.

Online

Gamban is software that can be installed on your devices to self-exclude you from international gambling websites and applications.

- *Gamban* offers a free trial and after this there is a monthly or annual subscription fee.
- The self-exclusion will remain in place for the duration of the subscription.
- For more information, visit: https://gamban.com/.

GAMSTOP is a website you can sign up to for free to self-exclude from UK gambling websites.

- You can self-exclude for either six months, one year, or five years.
- The self-exclusion will remain in place unless you ask to be removed.
- For more information, visit: www.gamstop.co.uk/.

Bookmakers

Multi-Operator Self-Exclusion Scheme (MOSES) is a self-exclusion service for bookmakers.

- MOSES allows you to self-exclude from multiple premises over the phone, without you needing to visit individual shops.
- Staff will help you identify the areas you are likely to visit to gamble and will use a mapping tool to add these to the exclusion.
- The self-exclusion will remain in place for one year and you can add more bookmakers at any point.
- For more information, visit: https://self-exclusion.co.uk/.

Casino

Self-Enrolment National Self-Exclusion Scheme (SENSE) is the self-exclusion service for casinos.

- You can self-exclude by speaking to the manager of the casino.
- They will request some basic details to register you on the SENSE scheme, and after this your accounts with all SENSE participating casinos will be closed.
- The self-exclusion lasts for a minimum of six months and will remain in place until you ask for it to be removed.
- For more information, visit: https://bettingandgamingcouncil.com/sense-self-exclusion-scheme.

Bingo

The Bingo Industry Self-Exclusion Scheme is the service used to self-exclude from bingo premises.

- You will need to complete a form either at your local bingo hall or online.
- After completing the form, staff will contact you to discuss the scheme in more detail and after this the self-exclusion will be complete.
- For more information, visit: www.bingo-association.co.uk/self-exclusion.

Arcades

Bacta, the trading body for amusement arcades, provides a self-exclusion service for their premises.

- You can self-exclude by contacting their self-exclusion helpline or speaking to staff at the arcade.
- The self-exclusion will last for six to twelve months and will remain in place until you ask for it to be removed.
- For more information, visit: https://bacta.org.uk/self-exclusion/.

Lottery

- *The National Lottery* allows you to self-exclude by changing the settings on your online account. For more information, visit: www.national-lottery.co.uk/responsible-play.
- You can also self-exclude from other lottery providers. For more information, visit the organisation's website or search their name and self-exclusion in a search engine.

'**Stimulus Control Strategies**' help you to consider many available strategies so you can choose those that are most likely to be of help to you.

Stimulus Control Strategies

Choose at least two stimulus strategies you can implement to reduce your access to money and gambling. If you already have strategies in place, identify at least one more you can introduce to limit your opportunities to gamble.

Reduce Access to Money

Only carry the exact money you need each day ☐
Do not carry spare money for emergencies ☐
Use Android or Apple pay instead of carrying cash ☐
Purchase vouchers for services you use ☐
Leave bank cards at home ☐
Order a new bank card and only use the contactless limit ☐
Order a new bank card and remove the security code on the back ☐
Hand over control of your bank account to someone else ☐
Set a withdrawal limit on your account ☐
Transfer spare money to a limited access savings account ☐
Have your salary or benefits paid into someone else's account ☐
Request someone else receives alerts from your bank when you spend ☐
Join a bank that allows you to block gambling transactions ☐

Reduce Access to Gambling

Install *Gamban* on your devices ☐
Sign up to *GAMSTOP* ☐
Sign up to MOSES ☐
Sign up to SENSE ☐
Self-exclude from bingo premises ☐
Self-exclude from your local arcades ☐
Self-exclude from the National Lottery ☐
Self-exclude from the Postcode Lottery ☐
Self-exclude from the Health Lottery ☐
Avoid visiting pubs, newsagents, etc. where you buy gambling materials ☐
Discuss restricting your access to gambling material or premises with
the manager or owner if self-exclusion is not possible ☐

Obstacles

Creating distance between you and the gambling is paramount and we recommend that you apply stimulus control before you start practising the remaining skills in this book. We, however, recognise that it's not always easy to do. Here is a list of the most common obstacles that could get in the way of applying stimulus control, together with ideas on how to overcome them:

- **No scheme available:** Unfortunately, there is not a self-exclusion scheme for all forms of gambling, such as scratch cards, pub machines, or spread betting. Therefore, it is particularly important that you limit your access to money as much as possible. It may also be a good idea to speak to the manager of these establishments and ask that they help restrict your use or purchase of gambling products.

- **Not fool-proof:** Stimulus control strategies are not fool-proof. You may find opportunities to gamble despite having controls in place. If you do, treat it as a learning experience and consider additional ways to overcome these barriers; think about what else you need to do to be safe from gambling. Applying stimulus control may be something that you need to build over time.

- **Inconvenience:** The strategies will likely inconvenience you. You will have less financial flexibility and everyday activities, such as grocery shopping, may require more planning. Making these changes will likely feel uncomfortable; however, discomfort is a sign that you are changing a long-standing behaviour.

- **Anxiety:** The thought of not being able to access gambling may be frightening. It may also feel overwhelming to think about how you are going to put these strategies in place. You could create a step-by-step plan of the strategies you would like to introduce and work your way through them one at a time. If you feel comfortable, you could also ask someone close to you for support.

- **Shame:** You may also feel ashamed admitting that you have a problem with gambling. Your gambling may have led you to be dishonest and you may feel guilty about the harm you have caused others. However, being open and honest is important in helping you break free from your gambling.

- **Losing independence:** Handing over financial control to someone else can be difficult. You may find that you struggle with this change and feel that you have lost your independence. But consider the alternative, at the moment it is too dangerous for you to have access to your own money. Through reducing your financial control, you can start to have more control over your gambling.

- **Motivation:** A part of you may want to leave the door half open to gambling, rather than closing it completely. Now that you have a better idea of what is involved in stopping or reducing your gambling, you may want to go back to Chapter 3 and complete the exercises again, being honest about how ready you are to stop.

How to Apply Stimulus Control

At the Clinic, we run a workshop on stimulus control strategies and members often help each other with ideas based on their own experiences. Use the examples below to think about stimulus control strategies that each individual can implement to limit their opportunities to gamble. As it often feels easier to help someone else, rather than ourselves, going through others' stories may help you think about how to overcome obstacles that may get in your way.

William's Story

William gambles nearly every day on football and horse racing. He used to go to the book-makers every weekend but has recently started gambling online. William has self-excluded from individual gambling websites but when he is determined to gamble, he will create a new account on a different website. William does not want his friends or family to know he has a problem as he feels ashamed.

What stimulus control strategies could William introduce to limit his opportunities to gamble?

_____

_____

_____

Amy's Story

Amy gambles every day on scratch cards and visits the casino once a week. She has been gam-bling more in the last three months and has recently spent all her wages at the casino. Amy has no stimulus control strategies in place. Her gambling is having an impact on her relationship with her partner and they are struggling to pay the bills. Amy's partner wants to help her but does not know how.

What stimulus control strategies could Amy introduce to limit her opportunities to gamble?

_____

_____

_____

_____

Skills Practice

1. Identify at least two stimulus control strategies that you could introduce to reduce your access to money and access to gambling (see '**Stimulus Control Strategies**').

2. Review the case studies and think about the strategies that these individuals could introduce to help limit their opportunities to gamble (see '**How to Apply Stimulus Control**').

3. Be prepared to overcome the obstacles that you may experience when introducing stimulus control strategies and acknowledge that changing a behaviour requires perseverance and commitment.

4. If you find that you are still able to gamble despite having stimulus controls in place, take some to reflect on the situation. Think about the strategies you are using, what is and is not helping, and make some changes to improve this.

Takeaway Points for Affected Significant Others

1. Taking the initial steps to introduce stimulus control strategies can be a challenge for individuals gambling problematically.

2. Stimulus control strategies may mean that the individual has less financial flexibility than usual. This may put limits on their everyday activities and activities may require much more planning than usual.

3. Stimulus control strategies are not fool-proof. If the individual is determined, they may find other ways to gamble. This can be hard for loved ones to understand, but humans are creatures of habit and it takes a lot of time and effort to change a behaviour.

4. Have a discussion with the individual and establish if there is anything you can do to help them set up these controls. If appropriate, you may wish to offer support with reducing their access to money.

5 How Gambling Hijacks Your Brain

Amanda Roberts and Steve Sharman

This chapter is about what happens to the brain when someone becomes addicted to gambling. It aims to help you understand better what you are up against when you try to break free from gambling. Because we are reviewing relevant research and theories, this book reads more technically than other chapters in the book. We are hoping that reading it will help you appreciate that you are up against a tricky brain. The skills covered in the rest of the chapters of this book are meant to help you re-train your brain. Applying the stimulus control, mentioned in the previous chapter, will help you 'buy' the time you need to re-train a tricky brain, taken over by gambling.

Research has shown that people who experience either gambling or drug addiction share similar alterations in the brain. As addiction develops, the brain changes as a response to 'highs' and develops 'cravings'. A physical withdrawal occurs when individuals attempt to stop gambling. This chapter will also look at the 'hooks' within gambling games that makes them so attractive.

To first understand what happens, we need to start with the anatomy of the brain itself.

Brain Anatomy

The brain is made up of hundreds of millions of cells called neurons. Neurons are connected to each other by a synapse which sends and receives messages about our feelings and behaviours through the release of a chemical called a neurotransmitter. The brain uses a lot of energy in this process – it is only 2% of body weight yet uses 20% of all food and water that we eat and drink.

Deep inside the brain, there are some systems and structures that control some important functions, such as the need for food and desire for sex. They are also involved in emotional responses like fear and anger through the production of hormones and the stimulation of neurotransmitters. One of these key systems is called the limbic system, and it is brain regions in this system that have been shown to be involved in gambling and disordered gambling. The limbic system controls some important functions, such as the need for food and desire for sex, but is also involved in gambling and disordered gambling.

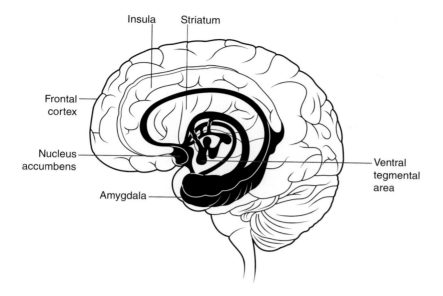

Within the limbic system, there are a series of areas that are important in the reward system, including the ventral tegmental area, the nucleus accumbens, and the insula. These areas are important in processes including the experience of basic positive and negative emotion, pleasure, and reward anticipation and feedback.

The Reward System

The reward system in our brains is wired so that when we do something that provides us with a reward, we tend to repeat that behaviour. From an evolutionary perspective, long ago, the reward system has developed to learn and adapt in this way to keep us alive; activities such as eating and sex cause the reward system to be activated, which makes us revisit these behaviours again to maintain and extend life.

Part of the role of the reward hub is to help recognise the cues that suggest when a reward may be coming. This part of the brain is activated when a reward is anticipated.

The subsequent pleasure associated with the activation of the reward hub makes you want to carry out the activity again. It is like when you were rewarded as a child for doing something right, dopamine would have been produced and the brain would have learned to perform that behaviour again.

Research shows the brain's pleasure and reward system is activated by gambling in a very similar way to how it is activated by drugs. Gambling can be a rewarding activity; a win can make you feel pleasure. Many gamblers talk about the 'rush' of the first win. That is the reward system being activated.

To experience these same feelings again, you may feel the desire to gamble again. And then again and again. This desire can be called craving. The main neurotransmitter involved here is dopamine.

Dopamine

Dopamine is also known as the 'happy chemical' and has two functions that are associated with addiction: rewards and learning.

Rewards: When you gamble, dopamine is released which makes you feel pleasure and satisfaction. The dopamine that is released in the reward pathways while gambling is higher than the amount natural rewarding experiences would generate (such as eating or having sex). People are originally attracted to gambling as it can be a highly rewarding experience.

Learning: Dopamine also helps us learn what makes us feel rewarded. The neurotransmitter encourages us to gamble again to achieve the same feeling. If we continue gambling, the brain will start to create 'shortcuts' in the neural pathways that connect the reward. This is because the brain does not have the capacity to think anew every time it meets a situation that requires some action. It needs a short-cut system, so it does not have to learn every time. It does this though something called plasticity.

It has been suggested that the brain functions by creating systems of loops – connections between cells that are strengthened by the brain in terms of how useful they are to the individual.

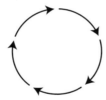

Loops that serve the person well are boosted; those that do not help are not boosted. The stronger loops would be used automatically when the individual encounters a similar situation. A loop is created between gambling and how it makes you feel. Gambling may be about pleasure, or for some it may be about dealing with pain.

For many individuals, the time when gambling was pleasurable may seem a distant memory. But gambling can still be performing a function for you; it may take your mind away from your current problems for a short while, or gambling may even be a way of getting rid of an uncomfortable urge to gamble.

However, often the brain works on a short-term basis – it can be a bit immature, taking a bit of pleasure now, even in the knowledge that there could be negative consequence in the long run. The brain has learnt that gambling can either take away some short-term pain or provide short-term pleasure.

Years of gambling has *reinforced* the belief that gambling can cure discomfort and/or give pleasure in the short term. This loop is very strong because it has been used so many times – apparently successfully. The more a loop is used, the stronger it becomes. The stronger it becomes; the more likely thoughts will flow through it.

Chapter 6 on rewarding yourself when you don't gamble and Chapter 9 about new activities to replace gambling are about helping your brain create a new loop.

The Competition

The question is often posed that there must be a loop that says 'gambling is bad' that has developed over the years? Why is this loop not the automatic one that is used? This is a good question.

The 'gambling loop' says that gambling is good; it competes with a smaller loop that says 'gambling is bad':

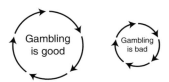

Why is the 'gambling is bad' loop so small? If the 'gambling is bad' loop is dominant, then it means you cannot gamble. If you cannot gamble, you might think you:

- Cannot enjoy gambling
- Will miss out on the chance of winning money
- Will be bored
- Will feel uncomfortable at trying to prevent gambling.

In the short-term, this loop does not do much for you, and it is the short-term that matters to the brain. The 'gambling is bad' loop relies on the understanding of the long-term gains at the expense of short-term discomfort. When you come across reminders of gambling, they can act as triggers, which activate the 'gambling is good' loop. You will learn more about triggers in Chapter 8.

When you become addicted to gambling, the changes in your brain will cause you to experience gambling differently, and as a consequence, your behaviour may change, or has changed, in some of the following ways.

Tolerance

We keep on gambling in an attempt to reproduce the sensation of pleasure, and the experience of reward. But after time, it takes more and more gambling to obtain that same feeling. Dopamine has less of an impact as your brain has become more tolerant.

The level of pleasure the individual experiences is reduced, so to achieve the same feeling of pleasure or 'rush' as before, a person will have to bet even more to make it more exciting – just like individuals who are addicted to drugs need higher doses to experience the same mood or feeling. However, the more the brain is stimulated, the more of a tolerance is built up. The more you do that activity the less your brain's reward system will respond as it did before and so there is a never-ending cycle of gambling even more with even higher stakes. No matter how much someone keeps gambling, that initial 'rush' will not come back.

Claire's Story

Claire had gambled for over ten years when she came to see us. In the first year, gambling would have given her a feeling of thrill. This was no longer the case, but she kept seeking for her initial rush by betting more money and gambling long hours in the hope that she would eventually re-experience the initial level of pleasure. If she only had another big win! If only the next spin would be more exciting than the last one! Once in a while, she would feel the excitement returning but it would not last long and it would not be as rewarding.

Withdrawal

Dopamine receptors continue to decrease, and the reward circuit becomes what is known as 'blunted'. Without dopamine, depression can occur as the brain tries to get back to normal.

When someone starts gambling, their baseline is 'normal', so the dopamine makes them feel good. As an addiction progresses, the baseline changes to feeling bad, so the dopamine released takes them from bad to normal, rather than normal to happy.

If the person tries to stop gambling, they may experience symptoms of withdrawal.

The withdrawal symptoms can be similar to those who are addicted to drugs and alcohol and can include psychological symptoms such as insomnia (lack of sleep), mood swings, depression, anxiety, and cravings, as well as physiological symptoms such as sweating, aches and pains, and increased heart rate. Chapter 7 focuses on feelings of craving and how to deal with them.

Although Claire now hardly enjoyed gambling, she would find it really hard to stay away from it. She described finding some comfort in the sound of roulette. She craved this sound. She felt low, bored, and empty when she did not gamble. She had dreams of gambling in the casino and then first thing in the morning she would think about the next time when she would be able to gamble.

So here lies the problem. Excessive gambling becomes normalised; tolerance means that the person cannot experience any dopamine pleasure anymore and they feel they must gamble to keep withdrawal and depression away. Excessive gambling can lead to loss; money, jobs, relationships, and friendships can all go.

Lower Impulse Control

Part of the brain called the prefrontal cortex controls decision-making, impulses, and thoughts. Think of it as the 'voice of reason' that looks at the risks and rewards to help us make decisions. It helps us avoid risky behaviour.

Gamblers are often thought of as being more impulsive than non-gamblers; indeed, gambling has previously been classified as an impulse control disorder. There are many different types of impulsivity, and those gambling heavily have been found to be more impulsive through impairments in motor inhibition (inability to inhibit a physical response), attentional inhibition (being easily distracted), and decision-making (often choosing first and reasoning later). The constant stimulation of dopamine makes the neural pathways in this part of the brain become weaker and the voice becomes quieter. This means that a person will stop listening to the 'voice of reason' and will not be able to control their impulses so well. Chapters 10 and 11 focus on what thoughts you have when you are in an impulsive 'hot' mode and how to move away from them.

As a measure of impulsivity, gamblers have been shown to prefer smaller, immediate rewards to larger, later rewards; therefore, the immediate excitement of placing a bet may supersede the later rewards that come from not gambling.

Genetic Predispositions

Some research suggests that certain individuals may develop an addiction because of genetic predispositions in the brain's reward system. Images of brain activity (by functional magnetic resonance imaging) in people with gambling and substance addiction show that they have less activity in the 'reward hub' of the brain when they are waiting for rewards which suggest that they may process rewards differently to others. This may mean that they may not be as excited by natural rewards and drawn to seek out rewarding activities which can include the highs of drug-taking and gambling so they feel pleasure or can escape.

As well as the reward hub, the other part of the brain that may be different is the medial prefrontal cortex (mPFC). The role of the mPFC is to inhibit or stop a response – rather like a 'brake'. This is important as it stops us charging ahead without pausing to consider the consequences. Research has shown that there is less activity in this part of the brain in those with gambling disorder, which results in people paying less attention to its signal when looking for pleasure. This means that these individuals may have difficulty stopping gambling and are more impulsive; they may be weighing up risk and reward and current versus long-term outcomes and consequences wrongly.

However, despite these studies, it is still unclear whether people already have differences in brain structure before gambling or if gambling changes the brain. It may be some combination of the two and research is still ongoing.

In-game 'Hooks'

Gambling games are designed in certain ways to hook our brains.

Uncertainty: Reward uncertainty plays a part in the appeal of gambling. When we gamble, there is uncertainty about winning or the size of the reward. Dopamine is also released by the synapses when the reward is uncertain. In fact, when a reward is anticipated, dopamine release increases. Constant experience of such uncertainty can change how a person responds to losing. In some individuals, losing money may become the trigger for the release of dopamine. In a gambler, that would mean that even though they are losing, they still have the urge to keep gambling.

Lights and Sounds: Gambling can be a feast for the senses, with flashing lights and sounds making it an immersive experience. Online studies have shown that lights and sounds may make individuals more likely to gamble, even when paired with uncertainty. In fact, cues that are associated with a win such as sounds make gamblers think they are winning more than they are (they overestimate). This encourages them to keep gambling longer and faster. In some forms of gambling, certain cues associated with wins are activated in non-win outcomes, which can fool the brain into processing the outcome as positive (win) instead of negative (loss).

Near Misses: Near-misses are when the gambler feels that the desired outcomes is *almost* obtained. These near-miss almost-wins stimulate parts of the brain that usually react to wins, and increase a person's wish to gamble more, especially in disordered gamblers. This response also encourages the gambler to feel they are constantly *nearly* winning, rather than repeatedly losing. Research has also shown that near-misses are physiologically more arousing than other non-win outcomes. Even though near-misses are often experienced as more unpleasant than other non-win outcomes, they can trigger a bigger desire to continue gambling.

Take a Minute to Think

Now you understand what has been going on deep inside your brain; a brain that has been hijacked by gambling. It may have been that your brain was wired in such a way that made you more prone to develop an addiction.

As you can see, even the gambling games themselves are designed in certain ways to hook our brains. The odds were stacked against you. It is you against a tricky brain.

Your brain now needs re-training so you can begin to build up your new life. Chapters 6 to 11 will take you through a step-by-step guide of how to break free from gambling. Chapters 12 and 13, focusing on lapses and future planning, are about how to maintain your abstinence in the longer term.

Skill Practice

1. Remember your brain has been hijacked by gambling and now needs re-training. It is you against a tricky brain.
2. Think about when you first started gambling – was it more pleasurable then? Can you pinpoint a time when it all started changing?
3. Have you stopped listening to your 'voice of reason'? Take the time to think through your actions, and the potential consequences, rather than acting without thinking
4. Think about the features of the forms of gambling you have engaged with, and how they can hook your brain.

Takeaway Points for Affected Significant Others

1. The brain's pleasure and reward systems are activated by gambling in a very similar way to how they are activated by drugs.
2. The brain has been hijacked by gambling and now needs re-training – this *can* be done with time, patience, and practising the skills found in this book.
3. The chemicals that have been released though gambling means that a person may have stopped listening to the 'voice of reason' and will not be able to control their impulses so well.
4. Gambling games are designed in certain ways to hook our brains.

6 Retraining the Brain: Rewarding Yourself

Georgina Luck

In the previous chapter you learnt about your brain and how it can be altered by gambling. You are up against a 'tricky brain' that has been hijacked by gambling and needs to be retrained so you can stop gambling and stay abstinent. A good way to do this is to reward yourself when you don't gamble; this is what this chapter will focus on.

Rewarding yourself for the days, weeks, and months that you don't gamble is a critical part of successful recovery. Rewards reinforce the behaviour of not gambling as well as making a gambling-free life more enjoyable and therefore something you are more likely to sustain. If life without gambling doesn't feel enjoyable then it will be much harder to maintain abstinence long term.

How Does Rewarding Myself Help My Recovery?

As you have seen in previous chapters, excessive gambling neurobiologically changes the reward pathway in your brain. In other words, how your brain processes rewards appears different to the brains of people who do not gamble. Retraining the reward part of your brain is important and is best done using regular rewards.

Let's go back to how your brain works, mentioned in Chapter 5, and how this is related to rewards.

Rewards have often been a part of our lives from a young age, as rewarding good behaviour increases the likelihood of that behaviour being repeated in the future. It is likely that at some point you found gambling pleasurable. This would have triggered a release of dopamine in your brain, as gambling would have acted as a reward. Rewards are a key part of training your brain as they trigger dopamine, making you feel happy and, in this case, make you go back to gamble again.

Rewarding yourself for not gambling will, over time, strengthen the part of your brain that tells you that not gambling is good and will gradually weaken the idea that gambling is pleasurable. Rewards need to be something you want and would enjoy that you will only allow yourself to have if you manage to not gamble for the agreed amount of time (be that days, weeks, or months).

How Do I Go About Rewarding Myself, and What Rewards Should I Choose?

Rewards are very personal; what is rewarding for one person may not be rewarding for another. Think about rewards that are realistic and that can become part of your life without too much hassle. Anything can be a reward. A key point here is that *you only reward yourself if you manage to stay away from gambling*. This point is essential for the success of this entire exercise.

Have a look at '**Rewards Schedule**' and note down some rewards of varying sizes that you could give yourself for every day, week, and month that you stay away from gambling. And yes, *you will only be entitled to these rewards if you don't gamble!* Pick your rewards wisely so you have an incentive to stick to this rule.

If you have already been abstinent from gambling for a while, it can feel odd to reward yourself daily for not gambling when you have already managed many gambling-free days. Instead, consider sticking to weekly and monthly rewards to keep your motivation strong and a focus on your recovery. The important thing is to make rewards work for you.

Take a Minute to Think

When it comes to the choice of suitable rewards, you may experience all sorts of dilemmas.

Do you pick rewards of monetary value? This could give you an incentive to save your money to spend it elsewhere. On the other hand, you may feel guilty for spending any money on rewards, because it feels self-indulgent and you feel like you don't deserve it, especially if you are in debt due to gambling.

Do you want to include others in your reward? Such rewards could include going out for dinner with your partner once a month, meeting up for an activity with friends, or taking your children on a day out. Of course, making others part of your reward could create other difficulties later down the line. We will discuss common barriers at the end of the chapter.

What Doesn't Count as a Reward?

A reward is not something that you *need* and is already part of your ordinary life. For example, an appropriate reward would be to go out for dinner to your favourite restaurant or order a takeaway if you didn't gamble that day, but not simply to have dinner that night.

Rewards Schedule

Small Rewards I Can Give Myself for Not Gambling for One Day

Examples: A walk at lunchtime, a sweet treat, your favourite food for lunch, playing an X-Box game, having a relaxing bath.

_____

_____

_____

Now make a contract with yourself:

'Every day I don't gamble I will give myself _____'

Remember to reward yourself tonight if you don't gamble today!
Now, if you don't gamble for longer periods, we want you to give yourself **a special reward**. For example, have a big reward planned each time you manage to not gamble for a whole week. This reward could be a special dinner out, a trip to the cinema, or a day out doing a fun activity with family or friends. Again, you need to spend some time drawing up a list of these special rewards. If you lapse and have one or more gambling days in the week, then you don't receive your special reward that week. Once you are back not gambling again, then the chance to receive the special reward for one week of abstinence returns.

Special Rewards I Can Give Myself for Not Gambling for One Week

_____

_____

When you succeed in not gambling for one month you need to reward yourself with **an extra special reward**. Again, think about what would work for you.

Extra Special Rewards I Can Give Myself for Not Gambling for a Whole Month

_____

_____

How Do Rewards Make Me More Likely to Stay Away from Gambling?
Now that we have thought a bit about why rewards are so important and what might work for you, let's look a little more at how rewards impact your gambling behaviour.

Through gambling regularly, a loop was formed in your brain telling you that _gambling is good_. Often gambling becomes less pleasurable over time and becomes something you want to stop. As your brain has been hijacked by gambling for so long, making this change can be really challenging.

The loop that tells you gambling is good has been used many times in the past and has taught your brain that gambling, at least in the short term, will make you feel good. The diagram below shows you how much smaller and weaker the loop in your brain is that tells you _gambling is bad_.

Adapted from: Petry, N. (2004). Pathological gambling: Etiology, comorbidity and treatment. Washington: American Psychological Association

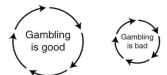

While this smaller loop reminds you of all the bad things about gambling, it has been used far less, mainly because in the heat of the moment our tricky brains tend to focus more on short-term pleasure more than long-term consequences. Now, it would be a good time to refer to the decisional balance (see '**Pros and Cons of Change**' in Chapter 3) to remind yourself of the pros and cons of your gambling habit.

Where do rewards come into this? There is a third loop, not mentioned yet.

Rewards will help strengthen a whole new loop in your brain: *not gambling is good*. This new loop helps to even out the imbalance between the existing loops and will be reinforced by the rewards you will give yourself for abstaining from gambling. By giving yourself something pleasurable for not gambling, this loop will become bigger and stronger as your brain learns that *not gambling is good*. The more immediate the reward, the better it will be at competing with the rewards that you used to enjoy when you gambled. It will also help you feel in your heart some of the pros of abstinence that you wrote down in your decisional balance.

It is important to note that retraining your brain to think differently about gambling requires **perseverance** and takes time! The key here is to replace the immediate enjoyment/pleasure that gambling offers with something else.

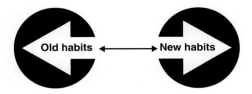

What Might Get in the Way of Rewarding Yourself?

Thinking of and putting rewards into practice is not something that everyone finds easy. Practical and financial difficulties, your own thoughts and feelings, and how others around you react to it can all make a difference.

Below, there are some of the most common obstacles that those who have attended the therapeutic programme in the National Problem Gambling Clinic have reported to us:

Nothing Else Works

Some people find it hard to think of things they want to reward themselves with. A common reason is that they do not enjoy anything as much as they enjoy/enjoyed gambling. Remember, gambling has hijacked the reward system in your brain, so it could take time before you start enjoying ordinary rewards.

List the things you used to enjoy before gambling became a problem. Maybe you used to go for a run twice a week, played tennis with a friend, or went on days out with your family. If you are struggling to think of something, have a look at the activity schedule in Chapter 9 for suggestions.

Realistically, it may be that nothing else will ever give you the same feeling that gambling did in the beginning. This is because gambling overloads the reward hub in your brain, meaning that other pleasant activities may not feel rewarding when you **first** try them after gambling has taken over, but the more you do them, the more rewarding they will feel.

Sean's Story

Sean is thirty years old and has been gambling since he was at university. Before gambling became a problem, he spent his weekends with his partner and his evenings playing football with his friends. Now that Sean is trying to pull away from gambling, he has committed to playing football after work with his friends once a week. Sean has chosen this reward as it is something that he used to enjoy. Committing to it will also help him feel motivated as he doesn't want to let his team down by not being able to go.

Not Deserving It

Some people may not feel as though they deserve a reward. This is often due to the negative impact that gambling has had on your life. Many people are left feeling guilty for their past actions, which can result in finding it hard to think about doing things that will make you feel good again. The key thing to remember is rewards will *increase the likelihood that you will be able to stay away from gambling*.

It may help to firstly remind yourself of the importance of rewards and then consider starting with smaller rewards to help you adjust to the idea of regularly rewarding yourself. Once you start to feel more comfortable and deserving of rewards you may want to add in newer or bigger rewards.

Since realising that his gambling had become a problem, Sean feels bad about what gambling has done to his life and doesn't' feel that he deserves to feel better in himself until he can fix everything. Sean knows how important rewards are to his recovery and is doing his best to push the guilty feelings aside and plan in rewards that will motivate him to stay away from gambling. When he reaches a new milestone in his recovery, he will also buy himself something tangible to remind him of how far he has come in his recovery.

Financial Cost of Rewards

It can feel hard to spend money, particularly if there has been a significant impact on your finances or you are in debt because of gambling. The key thing to remember is how important rewards are and to maybe think more about rewards that don't cost money. There are plenty of free rewards out there including a long bike ride, visiting a museum, or setting aside time to read or watch TV when you get home from work each day.

Ideally, you may want to push aside the guilt and see spending money on a reward as an investment in your recovery. Spending money on rewards will still save you money, as their cost will be less than gambling-related debts.

Sean started to feel bad that playing football was costing him money each week. Sean decided to focus on planning rewards that didn't cost him anything instead. He decided to schedule a long run every Sunday as his weekly reward and allocated himself an hour after work each day to watch an episode of his favourite TV programme. As Sean started to experience the benefit of rewards and re-train his brain, he realised that the cost of playing football would be really small in the long-run.

Others Judging You

It is common for those around you to also struggle with the concept of rewards. Often those who have witnessed the **negative consequences** of your gambling can find it hard to understand why you should be rewarding yourself, particularly if you are spending money. There are some points for family members and carers at the end of this chapter that can offer some advice and support. Sometimes sharing with those close to you **the rationale for rewards** and explaining to them how important it is as part of your ongoing recovery can help.

As Sean became more comfortable with rewarding himself, his partner was struggling to understand how he could justify rewarding himself when his gambling had had such a big impact on both of them over the years. Sean decided to show his partner this workbook and explain to them how important rewards are for his long-term recovery and how it might make them more part of his recovery if he were to schedule some rewards for them to do together. Have a look at the next point to see how he got on.

Including Others in Your Rewards

Some people like including others in their rewards and others don't. It may help **motivate you** if you are looking forward to an activity that you have planned with someone else as you know they will enjoy it too. It can also be a way of letting those around you know that you haven't gambled. On the other hand, some may find it anxiety provoking that if you were to gamble you would have to let the other person down. It may feel like you want to protect them, maybe at least in the early stages of recovery while you gain confidence.

Having spoken with his partner, Sean agreed that once a month he would plan in a reward for them to do together. They decided on a combination of dinners at their favourite restaurant once a month or day trip. Now Sean feels comfortable that if he were to, he would be able to tell his partner and cancel the reward. He also has a plan in place to go back to rewards that don't involve others if he starts to worry about letting his partner down in any way.

Rewarding yourself for not gambling can feel strange to both you and those around you but it is really important that you stick with it and remember rewards will only work if you choose things that have the potential to offer pleasure. It is the type of life that you lead when you have stopped gambling that will determine whether or not you maintain the gains. If your new gambling-free life is not pleasurable, cravings for gambling are far more likely to become stronger and threaten your recovery. Chapters 7 and 8 will be help you know how to handle cravings triggers and Chapter 9 how to carry on building a meaningful life.

Now you have read about the most common obstacles to putting rewards into practice, take some time to fill in 'Reflections on and Obstacles to Rewards Schedule'. This is about reflecting on how you feel about rewards, others' reactions, and any difficulties you anticipate. To overcome barriers, remind yourself of the long-term positive consequences of a reward system, push aside guilt and judgements, think how you would talk to a friend whom you really care about, consider getting a significant other on board with the idea of rewards so you have some support, and finally draw on any of the above ideas that seem relevant to you.

Most importantly, be honest and open with your feelings. It's ok not to be fully convinced yet. We, however, encourage you to give it your best shot before deciding if this is right for you.

Reflections on and Obstacles to Rewards Schedule

How do you feel about the idea of rewarding non-gambling behaviour?

_____

_____

_____

_____

_____

How will others around you react to the idea of rewards?

_____

_____

_____

_____

_____

What obstacles can you see preventing you from implementing your rewards and how might you overcome them?

Obstacles

1. _____

2. _____

3. _____

Overcoming Obstacles

1. _____

2. _____

3. _____

Skills Practice

- Come up with a list of small daily rewards – you can only give these rewards to yourself if you **don't** gamble.

- Then choose some slightly bigger rewards to be used weekly or monthly – again only when you don't gamble (remember to include others in your rewards if you wish).

- Identify what obstacles can get in the way of this exercise and think how you will address them.

Takeaway Points for Affected Significant Others

- We ask those affected by gambling to start rewarding themselves for the days, weeks, and months when they don't gamble.

- This may sound like a strange thing to ask given that gambling may have caused harm to your loved one(s) and the people around them.

- We however try to re-train a tricky brain and help it learn that gambling is bad and not gambling is good.

- You are entitled to have your own feelings about this technique, and you may want to support your loved one(s) with it or not.

Hopefully, in the long run the benefits of reward will outweigh any cost.

7 Coping with Cravings and Urges

Antony Malvasi

This chapter focuses on different ways to handle cravings and urges to gamble. It may seem strange to talk about cravings in the context of gambling as we usually associate them with drugs, alcohol, or food. However, even though gambling is a non-chemical activity, similar chemical processes take place as with drugs, alcohol, or food. In fact, research shows that individuals with a gambling problem experience stronger cravings and find it harder to resist them, as compared to those with alcohol or cocaine dependency.

In the National Problem Gambling Clinic, we have met many individuals, initially saying that they don't experience cravings. However, when it is explained to them what we mean by cravings, and they start to pay attention, they begin to recognise that they actually do have cravings, especially when they try to stop. Identifying and managing cravings can be a key factor in preventing a lapse.

What Are Cravings?

Cravings refer to the range of thoughts, feelings, and sensations that usually occur before you gamble or when you try to stop. They can range from mild edginess, agitation, or restlessness to full-blown anxiety such as sweating, sickness in the stomach, and heart racing. Some people report a state of mild euphoria, excitement, or even a sense of relief or hope.

Cravings can also appear in the form of 'gambling-related' thoughts, or anticipatory thoughts about winning, which you will read more about in Chapters 10 and 11. Some people slip into a dialogue between their thoughts about why they should and why they shouldn't gamble. Other people report thoughts of hopelessness at being able to resist the urge.

What Is Going On?

It can be very frustrating to be dead set on not gambling one minute and then find yourself coming up with justifications to gamble the next despite being aware of the harmful consequences. It seems irrational and makes no sense to keep doing something which is harmful to you, but the answer lies in a brain chemical known as 'dopamine', which is associated with reward and gives you a feeling of well-being. We have already mentioned it in Chapters 5 and 6. Dopamine is released when you have a gambling win and over time, even when you are reminded of gambling. The brain has become so used to receiving large supplies of dopamine through gambling that it wants to continue to experience this feeling of reward; so, it creates discomfort in the form of cravings in order to make you continue to gamble so you can experience relief from them. Your brain is not out to harm you, far from it; it just has its wires crossed about what is and isn't good. The brain is wired to obtain short-term gains as much as possible and is governed by quest for pleasure.

In essence, when you gamble, not only are you activating the reward pathways of the brain, you are also stimulating the deeper structures, known as the 'limbic' system, which is associated with our vital physiological processes such as eating, drinking, and sex. Therefore, cravings can feel so powerful and make you feel like gambling is something you need and can't survive without rather than a want – we would not be able to survive without food, water, and sex. However, as unpleasant as an urge may feel, it will only last several minutes at the most and you WILL survive if you don't give into it. There are also many other ways to obtain dopamine, as discussed in Chapter 6.

How to Recognise Cravings

So, the brain, in order to continue to feel good via dopamine, does everything in its power to get you to continue gambling even when you want to stop. It's YOU versus a tricky brain! So, you should know what tricks your brain is going to come up with.

1. Gambling-related Thoughts

Your brain's first response will be to try to find reasons to justify continuing to gamble – it looks for excuses, or gambling-permissive thoughts, which you will find out more about in Chapter 10. Some of these thoughts will first appear reasonable and rational as the brain needs reasons why it should act against other competing thoughts about not gambling. Other thoughts may be about anticipated positive effects of gambling or the intensity of your craving.

Take a Minute to Think

Some of the more commonly reported excuses, which appear as gambling-related thoughts, are:

I am going to win this time

It's only £5

I will gamble once and leave

I had such a terrible day – gambling will help me forget all about it

I can't function without gambling

My desire to gamble is so overpowering. I can't think of anything else

Can you think of any other gambling-related thoughts that you've had?

2. Emotions

A second strategy your tricky brain uses is playing a version of 'good cop, bad cop' with you – if you gamble, you get dopamine, if you stop you get hormones like adrenaline, which make you feel anxious. If you finally gamble, then the brain shuts off the adrenaline, or it is perceived as being a part of the 'thrill' or 'rush' that people describe. So, emotions, such as anxiety, excitement, and euphoria, could all be part of feelings of craving.

3. Physical Sensation

Gambling or just thinking about gambling can set off various physiological reactions in your body. Many individuals report feeling palpitations, increase in temperature, increase in heart rate and pulse, stomach churning, sweating, quickening and shortening of breath, and tension in the body; this can vary according to the individual. Once you start to pay more attention to your body, you will get better at recognising your particular physiological reactions.

Ed and Pete's Story

Ed had been gambling for several years and every time he walked past a bookmakers he would immediately start thinking about the odds on the horses and what bets he could place; he would get anxious and excited at the same time, experiencing sweaty palms, heart pounding, and shallow breathing and butterflies in his stomach.

Pete, on the other hand, would regularly experience tension headaches because he would worry about his debts and then think about what bets he was going to place to win money to pay them off. He would regularly clench his jaw without realising it and carried a lot of tension in his shoulders. If Pete hadn't gambled for a few days, he would find himself getting very irritable and restless and without knowing that this was part of having cravings, he would gamble, and even if he lost, he would feel some sense of relief.

Now you have a better idea of what a craving looks like, start monitoring your cravings, using 'Catching a Craving'. The faster you can catch a craving, the easier it will be to apply coping strategies.

Catching a Craving

Situation	Thoughts	Emotions	Physical sensations	How intense was the craving? (1–100) How long did it last?
Tuesday evening — TV advert	I have missed placing a bet	Anxious Excited	Heart palpitations Sweaty palms	80/100

How to Cope with Cravings

Now that you have some idea about what is going on, the next step is to have some tools to help to you deal with cravings so that you do not lapse back to gambling. The following are some suggestions to help you deal effectively with a craving until it passes.

Surf the Wave

One of the most important things to remember about a craving is that it only lasts for a limited period and that no matter how bad it feels, IT WILL PASS. Imagine that it is like a wave, steadily rising, reaching a peak for several minutes and then fading away. It is during this peak that you are most vulnerable because this is when the craving is most powerful and this is when you are most likely to act on it, so the earlier you can spot the craving the better. One of the techniques we recommend is 'urge surfing'.

Here is what you do. When you experience a craving, acknowledge it to yourself first, 'I am having a craving', and then imagine yourself riding a wave like a surfer. Observe how the craving feels in your body and mind, going with it rather than re-sisting it and tell yourself that you WILL NOT gamble for a period of time. Choose a time interval that you can commit to where you are 100% confident you will not gamble (even if this is only a few minutes). At the end of that time, again decide to postpone the decision to gamble for a further interval that you are confident you can achieve. Eventually, after a period, the dopamine system will stop functioning and the urge to gamble will fade.

Each time you practise this and succeed, you will build your confidence at man-aging your cravings and you will no longer be afraid of them. Over time, the association between cravings and gambling will become weaker and weaker, and eventually they will disappear. If cravings continue, then the chances are that you are still exposed to the stimulus that cued the urge in the first place and you need to either find a way to get away from it or find a way to protect yourself from the stimulus.

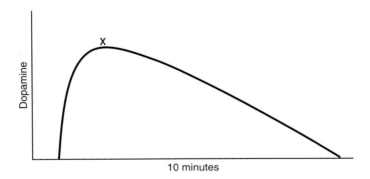

Some things that might get in the way of successfully 'urge surfing' are judging yourself for having a craving in the first place, which can make you feel worse and put you in a negative frame of mind, making it more likely that you will give up too quickly. 'Urge surfing' is like everything else, the more you practice it, the better at it you will get. Another obstacle might be that rather than staying in the moment and observing the craving, you start to think about the future and wonder how you are going to get through the day or the week. Just keep directing your attention to the present moment and the next few minutes, keeping the task small and more immediate, and once you get through the first several minutes you are more likely to succeed.

Ride the wave and master your craving!

Self-soothing Techniques

The process of stopping gambling can be extremely stressful and frustrating due to the lack of dopamine and the adrenalin produced; this can cause severe anxiety which causes shortness of breath and muscle tension, putting you into a state of discomfort and making it very difficult to think clearly. Therefore, learning how to relax and put yourself into a calm state is a key essential skill in the recovery process. The following techniques help slow down your brain, reducing your anxiety and tension by putting you into a different part of the nervous system, away from the 'fight or flight' response by triggering the relaxation response. This is about doing something comforting, nurturing, and gentle for yourself to help put you into a relaxed, calm state so that you can think clearly, and then you are more likely to respond constructively from this place of clarity and calmness.

Involving your senses: One way of doing this is by focusing on one of your senses, such as looking at a pleasing picture or photograph in a book or going to a gallery perhaps, or going for a pleasant walk. You may try to find some pleasant sounds – listen to a calming piece of music, or pick some sounds out of your environment to focus on like rain or wind. Do something that soothes your skin, like taking a hot bath or shower, or stroking a pet, put on a woolly jumper or lie in fresh bedclothes. You might want to eat or drink something nice, just something small that you like and can savour as you taste it.

Relaxation: Any sustained focused attention on the breath is a great way to help shift you from an anxious mind state to a more relaxed and calm mind state. When we get anxious, the muscles around our rib cage and chest can really tighten up and our breath can become really shallow and quick as if in a panic state. The problem here is that you are not giving your lungs a chance to empty themselves out properly and it can literally feel like you are drowning. To counteract this, try the following exercise which is a combination of breath and body awareness.

Instructions: Twenty-minute Practice

(Listen to a recording or ask someone to read out the text below in a calm and soothing voice.)

Firstly, find somewhere quiet, peaceful, and private. Sit or lie down and make yourself as comfortable as possible. If you are sitting, try not to slump and sit as straight as possible. Have your back supported if necessary or you can sit on the floor with your back against the wall. You could sit in a chair or crossed leg on a cushion. If you are lying down, find a neutral space such as the living room floor rather than your bed (unless you want to do this exercise before going to sleep). You are trying to cultivate a sense of 'relaxed alertness'.

To begin with, just spend some time getting to know your breath. Make your breath the most important thing for the next several minutes. Place your attention on the inhalation and the exhalation (1 min). Get to know your breath intimately. Observe the length of the inhalation compared to the length of the exhalation (1 min). Notice where you feel the movement first in your body as you breathe in and out (30 secs). Notice how the body expands as you breathe in and contracts as you breathe out (30 secs). Notice how the rib cage expands and contracts as you breathe in and out (30 secs). Notice how the air is cool when you breathe in and notice how it is warm as it leaves your body (30 secs). Notice how the belly expands and contracts as you breathe in and out (30 secs).

Sometimes, it is helpful to count the length of the inhalation. Do so if you wish. Breathe in for 1 and 2 and 3 … … and then count the length of the exhalation. Breathe out for 1 and 2 and 3 … and so on (1 min). Don't try to change anything. Just observe each breath as it enters and leaves your body moment by moment (2 mins). Notice that there are four parts to the breath: there is a natural pause at the end of the inhalation and there is a natural pause at the end of the exhalation. Rest your awareness in the pause after each breath and notice what happens (2 mins). You may notice that just by paying careful, loving, kind attention to your breath in this way that it slowly starts to deepen and lengthen and even itself out, finding a greater equilibrium (2 mins).

Don't be put off if you find that your mind initially becomes more active and is distracted by thoughts, making it difficult to focus. Acknowledge each thought and gently bring your attention back to the breath. When another thought arises, acknowledge it and let it go without judging yourself. Just let everything be as it is (2 mins). If a feeling arises again, acknowledge it and let it go; whatever you notice arising in your consciousness accept it and let it go without judging (it could be anxiety, boredom, impatience, tiredness, self-judgement – 'I am no good at this'); embrace all of it (2 mins). Try not to pursue the thought or push it away as it is part of the now, part of this moment. Acknowledge it and let it go and gently bring your attention back to the breath (1 min).

Let your field of your awareness now expand to include your body and notice any physical sensations in your body; any aches or pains that have arisen; any parts of your body that feel hot or cold; the contact your sitting bones make with the floor or chair; the position of your spine in relation to your pelvis; the position of your head in relation to your spine; notice the contact the air makes with your skin, your face; observe all of it without judging it or trying to push it away; embrace all of it as part of your experience and what is going on in this moment. Moment by moment. Breath by breath (1 min). Slowly start to bring your awareness back into the room as we start to come to the end of our meditation on the breath and the body. Tune into the sounds around you. Feel the temperature in the room. And gently open your eyes when you are ready (1 min).

Reaching Out

Texting or talking to someone is another good technique. It is useful to have a few designated people that you have thought about beforehand that you know you can call when you are experiencing a craving. Many gamblers keep their urges secret, so as not to worry or burden others or because they feel ashamed or guilty. But which is more worrying – being honest or risking more gambling losses?

'I did it! I did it! I mastered a craving!'

The other person doesn't have to give you advice; sharing about how you feel can be enough to snap you out of the craving state and start to think more consciously again. You could also attend a support group or find a chat forum. See '**Complete Your Own Personal Crisis Plan**' in Chapter 13, which asks you to make a list of people that you could seek help from, if you felt the urge to gamble.

Avoid the Trigger

If you can avoid or remove yourself from whatever it is that is making you think about gambling, then do so: if it is gambling premises, walk the other way; if it's a website, shut the computer down and leave the room; if it's another gambler, don't mix with them. Chapter 8 on triggers helps you to recognise your triggers and learn how to deal with them better – avoiding them completely is a way of protecting yourself from them and feelings of craving.

Physical Activities and Distraction

Some people may need to do something more physical to help distract them from a craving such as exercise or going for a walk. Try to completely immerse yourself in what you are doing so as not to think about gambling. Chapter 9 is about activities that you could engage in as a way of enriching your life but also battling cravings.

Responding to Thoughts

You must watch out for 'gambling-related' thoughts as discussed above. Chapters 10 and 11 focus on how to catch these thoughts early and how to respond back in a way that could help you resist any urges to gamble.

Final Remarks about Craving

Coping with cravings is a necessary and inevitable part of the recovery process. Changing any long-term ingrained behaviour is challenging and uncomfortable in the beginning; however, if you practise the techniques discussed above, and keep practising and persevering, you will see that gradually you will be able to master and overcome cravings until they completely disappear. Eventually, the process of mastering your cravings and your recovery process will become rewarding in itself as you clock up your days of abstinence and the rewards that go with it! Use '**Coping with Craving**' to record what coping strategies you practised to deal with cravings.

Take a Minute to Think

- People can often feel disappointed too quickly because they tried the strategies a couple of times and they did not work.

- Take a minute to ask yourself – how long have you gambled for? Depending on your answer, think about what may be a realistic timeframe for you to deal with your cravings and then apply the time, effort, and persistence.

- Learning to cope with craving is like learning to swim. Don't wait until you start drowning in order to practise. Start practising at least a couple of the above strategies daily or as often as you can, even if you do not experience cravings. Then you will find it easier to apply them when you need them the most.

- If you find that some of the above strategies do not work for you after having given them your best shot, then stick with those that you found helpful.

So just keep practising and keep reminding yourself that the recovery process takes a little longer and is the opposite of instant gratification: short-term pain for long-term gain! And that it will all be worth it in the end to live a gambling-free life!

Coping with Craving

Situation	Intensity (1–100)	Length of craving	Which coping strategy did you practise?
Tuesday evening — TV advert	80/100	15 mins	Surf the wave — waiting for the craving to pass WhatsApp messages to my friend

Skills Practice

- The first step to master your cravings is to become aware of them. Monitor and record the type and intensity of craving you had.

- Pick any one of the coping strategies discussed and try it out regularly in the coming week. When you have mastered a strategy, practise another one.

- Surf the wave, self-soothing and relaxation, and reaching out to others are some of the strategies covered in this chapter.

Takeaway Points for Affected Significant Others

- It can be helpful for your loved one to have someone to turn to for support when they are having a craving.

- You could remind them that the craving will eventually pass and that nothing bad will happen to them if they don't give in to the craving.

- It can be helpful to your loved one to ask them what they need and perhaps offer them a hug or a massage, go for a walk together, or practise another strategy covered here.

- Keep reminding them how well they are doing and how it will all be worth it in the end.

8   'Catching' and Limiting Triggers Early

Dolors Manuel-Riu

In this chapter you will learn to be more aware of triggers that put you at risk of gambling so that you can 'catch' them early and use new strategies to cope with them.

What Are Triggers?

A trigger is something that comes before a gambling episode or something that threatens your sense of control and makes it more likely for you to consider gambling. Different people will have their own set of specific situations, strong feelings or thoughts that make them want to gamble. When you are aware of your triggers you can foresee risk and put strategies in place to stop you from gambling.

In this chapter you will spend some time thinking about your individual triggers and consider the strategies you can use to cope with them. The coping strategies covered in this chapter as well as those found in Chapters 7 and 11 are all meant to form part of your repertoire of means to resist gambling urges.

Triggers can be very subtle, and can take some time and thought to uncover. A memory of winning, boredom, low mood, or feeling lucky can all be triggers to gamble. Some of these might not be immediately obvious as triggers but they create circumstances under which you are more likely to gamble. Any of the above events could trigger a gambling thought and if you have access to gambling (cash, bookmakers, and online accounts) then you run the risk to gamble. Equally, unexpected access to cash or to a gambling opportunity could make you think about gambling when you did not intend to.

Triggers are often subtle, making them easy to miss. Thus, the first step is to learn to recognise a trigger EARLY; the earlier you do, the more time you have to implement coping strategies.

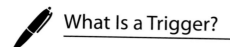# What Is a Trigger?

This is a list of events and situations that could act as triggers. They can remind you of gambling and perhaps spark the desire to gamble, even when you did not actively intend to do so.

Examples of Triggers

- You've had a tense or bad day
- You are anxious or worried
- You are bored, or have spare time on your hands
- You are in a social situation linked to gambling
- You feel bad about yourself or guilty about something you have/have not done
- You are depressed
- You want to feel energised or 'high'
- You want to test your willpower
- You feel a physical need or urge to gamble
- You feel like blowing up because of frustration
- You feel everything is going wrong for you
- You feel angry
- You are on holiday and want to relax and have fun
- You can see others gambling
- You have just been paid
- You are receiving gambling offers via text/email
- You have had/are drinking alcohol
- You were given a pay rise
- You have inherited money
- You are seeing adverts on TV
- You are walking past a bookmaker
- You are in town
- Your partner is away for the evening
- You are watching sport

Which of the Above Situations Has Acted as a Trigger for You?

1. _____

2. _____

3. _____

4. _____

5. _____

Identifying My Triggers

Now that you may have gained a clearer idea of what triggers are, the next exercise is to help you to focus more on the triggers that place YOU more at risk of gambling.

 Take a Minute to Think

In order to help you identify your triggers, we prompt you to break them down in particular groups. Triggers can be about:

1. People
2. Places
3. Events or times of day or year
4. Thoughts and feelings

Think about the last times that you gambled or when you felt like gambling. What was it that set it off? What was happening? Where were you? How were you feeling?

The more triggers you can identify now, the more prepared you will be to 'catch' them in real time, so it's worth investing some time in creating an exhaustive list of your triggers.

My Triggers to My Gambling

People	Places
<ul><li>Someone reminding you of gambling?</li><li>Someone talking about it or asking you to join in?</li><li>Someone who makes you feel stressed, annoyed, sad …?</li></ul>	<ul><li>Particular routes to work?</li><li>Certain high streets?</li><li>Certain rooms in the house?</li></ul>
Thoughts/feelings	**Events/times**
<ul><li>Are there thoughts that give you permission to gamble? i.e.: only one bet, only £10</li><li>Do you ever visualise winning – or how you are going to spend the money?</li><li>Do you recall past wins?</li><li>Are there feelings that come before gambling thoughts?</li><li>Are you bored? Angry? Depressed?</li><li>Do you have the desire to block negative emotions?</li></ul>	<ul><li>Pay day?</li><li>Lunchtimes?</li><li>After work?</li><li>First thing in the morning, the minute shops open?</li><li>After pubs close?</li><li>When your partner goes to bed?</li><li>Weekends?</li><li>Football matches?</li><li>When drinking?</li></ul>

Why Is It Important to Be Aware of Triggers?

When you are faced with a trigger you are more likely to gamble if you have not prepared in advance on how to deal with it. Triggers can cause you to switch to 'automatic' mode, in which you act out of habit without thinking. Thus, you could end up making a chain of decisions that bring you closer to gambling without you even realising.

Becoming aware of your triggers and using foresight allows you to **stop, think**, and **do something different** *instead* of gambling. This allows you to break the gambling cycle and feel more confident about your abstinence. Looking at Carl's story below will make this clearer.

Carl's Story

Carl has not gambled for over a month. He is meeting some friends at the pub today. It's a lovely sunny Saturday morning and he is feeling good. His friends will be watching the Wimbledon final. Carl likes tennis and is wondering who the champion will be this year. He leaves his house far in advance, so that he has plenty of time to walk to the pub. He takes his bank card with him, although he had been very strict about leaving it at home until recently. On the way he passes by a bookmaker and looks at the tennis odds on the window display. He decides to enter and place a bet. Carl says to himself that it will only be a small bet and that after all, his problem was the Fix Odd Betting Terminal (FOBT) machines, and he was never into sports betting. Once he has placed the tennis bet, he walks past the FOBT machines and decides that it's still early and he could just play a couple of spins. He thinks he could make some money to buy drinks for his friends. He starts playing and ends up losing £150. His mood has dropped. He is now late, angry, and not in the mood to meet his friends. He leaves and goes back home.

Carl felt awful about what happened and his day was ruined. Unfortunately, he was not aware of a series of triggers and the decisions he made without thinking through their risks.

Can You Spot the Triggers on Carl's Chain of Events?

Can you spot the decisions he made in 'autopilot' mode?

Carl faced the following triggers:

- It was a sunny leisurely Saturday morning (time)
- It was the Wimbledon final (event)
- He was feeling good (feeling)
- He had access to money (event)
- He passed by a bookmaker (place)
- He thought he was in control (thought)
- He entered the bookmakers (place)
- He thought he was safe to place a sports bet (thought)
- He saw FOBT machines (place)

Let's start by looking at the decisions that Carl made and what he could have done to protect himself if he had been more aware of his triggers.

Leaving the House with Spare Time

Free time before meeting his friends was risky for Carl. He could have coped with this risk by asking a friend to pick him up, leaving the house later, or driving to the pub.

Carl Took His Bank Card with Him

Carl had been leaving his bank card at home until now. It was very risky to take it with him that day, as there was a big sports event on and he was going to the pub to watch it. He should not have taken that risk unless he had controls on his bank card. He could also have taken a small amount of cash instead of his bank card.

Carl Took a Route That Passed by a Bookmaker

Bookmakers were a big trigger for Carl as he had not excluded himself from his local bookmakers when he decided to stop gambling. Using a different route may have helped him avoid gambling-related thoughts.

Carl Decides that It Is Safe to Place a Sports Bet

Carl's 'permission-giving thought' tells him that he is in control and safe to place only one bet. Carl could have recognised this thought as an 'excuse' that his brain generates, as explained in Chapter 10, and used some of the techniques found in Chapter 11 about managing this thought differently.

There was a chain of events that led Carl to gamble and he did not seem aware of the risks he was taking. The closer he came to lapsing, the harder it became to get out of the situation. Once Carl was inside the bookmakers his brain was on 'auto-pilot', flooded with dopamine and generating permission-giving thoughts. It was almost impossible to access his rational brain, challenge his actions, and leave the premises without gambling.

This is why it is important to catch your triggers early. The earlier you act the better your chances of success. It allows you to **stop, think, and put a strategy in place**.

'Catching' My Triggers

Having read Carl's story, you may be left wondering how you could have done better and been able to spot your triggers early. Catching the trigger early is half the battle. The **'Triggers Diary'** exercise could help you practise uncovering your triggers and so getting better at noticing them, but also at observing any coping strategies that have helped you deal with them.

Triggers Diary

Use this triggers diary to record the triggers you come across during the week.

This is a brief example of what your diary may look like:

Trigger Diary

Date	Trigger When, where, how? What was happening? How was I feeling? What was I thinking?	Did I gamble?	If yes: How did I feel afterwards? If no: How did I manage? What did I do that helped?
Example *12/2*	It was payday. I was thinking about my money in my account and that I could just place a couple of bets.	No	My partner now has access to my bank account. She would have known if I had gambled. I went for a run to distract myself.
14/2	I was paid some cash. Nobody knew about that money. Stopped at bookmakers on the way home	Yes	Felt 'bad' afterwards as I lost the money.

It can be useful to complete your diary at the end of every day, taking a few minutes to reflect on any urges that you may have had and what was happening at that time. You may also prefer to do it throughout the day, pausing to fill it in when the triggers are still fresh in your memory.

You may think that writing triggers down will make them more real and therefore make you more likely to gamble. This is a common thought, but we know that the opposite is true; it's when you are unaware of your triggers that you are most at risk to gamble. You may also be worried that someone will find your diary. Try to find a safe place to keep it or even complete it electronically.

Date	Trigger When, where, how? What was happening? How was I feeling? What was I thinking?	Did I gamble?	If yes: How did I feel afterwards? If no: How did I manage? What did I do that helped?

Managing My Triggers

Now that you have identified what triggers are risky, you can learn how to deal with them more effectively. It can feel overwhelming doing this for many triggers all at once, so it's easier to work on each one individually.

There are **three ways of handling triggers**. These are:

1. Avoid the triggers. Some situations can be easily avoided and this is the best way to cope with them. With Carl, for example, having access to money and passing by the bookmakers were his main triggers. Carl could have pre-arranged cash withdrawal limits and gambling restriction controls on his bank card or left it at home. He could have also excluded himself from local bookmakers.

Which triggers can I avoid?

- Can I pay at a counter where they don't sell scratch cards or avoid going into the newsagent?
- Can I have someone to hold my money when I am being paid?
- Can I make sure I can't access gambling websites on my phone, laptop, and computer?

2. Actively re-arrange your environment so that you are less likely to encounter your triggers. Leaving his house with time to spare and choosing a route passing by a bookmaker contributed to Carl's lapse. In order to minimise his risk, Carl could have asked a friend to pick him up or he could have left later and have chosen a different route if possible.

What can I change around me so that I will be less likely to gamble?

- How can I stop looking at the football results on my phone?
- How much cash do I really need to carry with me?
- Do I need to take my card with me when I go out?

3. Be prepared by developing new coping methods. Not all triggers can be avoided, especially thoughts or emotions. Often strong emotional states can act as triggers and for some people gambling is an opportunity to escape from everyday stresses and problems. For Carl, being in a good mood on a sunny Saturday morning and thinking that a small bet would not hurt acted as triggers. A cue card (see Chapter 4) could have helped Carl remember his reasons for not going ahead with his impulse.

What can I do instead of gambling? What would help me in this situation?

- What would make me feel better when I am stressed or angry? (Go for a run, exercise, walk, watch TV, …)
- What would help me feel better when I am feeling low? (Talk to a friend, listen to my favourite music, watch a film, go for a walk …)
- What can I do when I get calls from my creditors? (Speak to the debt agency, make a realistic plan and start making small payments …)
- What are the negatives of gambling?
- Can I reward myself instead of gambling with something soothing or pleasurable?

Here is a brief example on how to break your triggers down and how to cope with them.

Managing My Triggers

My trigger	What can I do to avoid this trigger? What can I do to make it less risky? How can I cope with it?
I keep receiving emails about gambling offers. It makes me think that I could just gamble the free money offered to me.	• I will block the website • I will clear my cookies from the browser • I will install gambling-blocking software • I will make sure that I delete any gambling information straight away without reading it • I will remember that once I start gambling, I can't stop and it's never going to be 'just the free money'
When I am very stressed and anxious, I gamble to block out my problems.	• I can exercise or do something physical to help me relax • I will focus on something practical I can do about my problem • I will ask myself: 'How is gambling going to help me in this situation?' • I will remember that I will feel worse after the gambling

Managing Triggers

Use this worksheet to generate strategies to cope with your triggers

My trigger	What can I do to avoid this trigger? What can I do to make it less risky? How can I cope with it?

Skills Practice

- Spend some time identifying your main triggers using '**What Is a Trigger**' and '**My Triggers to My Gambling**'. Try to identify what situations are riskier for you.

- Using your '**Trigger Diary**', spend some time during the week 'catching' and noting your triggers down.

- Think what strategies you can use to manage these triggers. What existing strategies are working well for you? If none, can you try something different?

- Remember to avoid risky situations if it's possible. Rearrange your environment and don't be afraid to try new things.

Takeaway Points for Affected Significant Others

- Urges and thoughts to gamble are unavoidable, especially when you first stop gambling. Certain things that have been associated with gambling can act as triggers.

- Encourage an open and honest conversation so that you can become aware of the things that trigger their desire to gamble.

- You can help limit triggers by having control of money and installing software on home devices to block gambling websites.

You can also help by being available for support when they experience strong urges to gamble.

9 Things to Do When You Don't Gamble

Venetia Leonidaki

This chapter is about how to enjoy life more *without gambling*. For many individuals with a gambling problem, gambling feels like it is the only pleasurable activity that they do. For some it is the only activity, pleasurable or not.

Something that is common to all addictive behaviours is that they begin as part of your life and end up taking over. That is, where you would occasionally spend time gambling or thinking about gambling, over time this starts to make other interests and activities disappear from your life. Without realising it, gambling has probably replaced most things that you once did. It may even be hard to imagine what is left there when you take the gambling away.

No-man's Land

Most people attending our clinic wish that gambling would be gone from their lives. They are aiming for a gambling-free life. However, that life needs building. This section is still relevant for those attempting to reduce gambling; there still needs to be a more general lifestyle change to achieve this.

When you first stop gambling, you may find yourself in a no-man's land and feelings of dullness, sadness, fear, or irritability may crop up. You are trying to leave your gambling behind and move towards building up a new life. This transition can take weeks or months. You are trying to break away from a familiar and exciting habit without yet having a new routine or something else to replace it with.

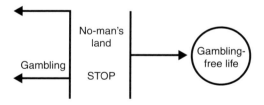

Finding new hobbies may be central to overcoming your gambling problem. The greater the number of pleasant activities in a person's life, the more often he/she experiences positive feelings – and fewer pleasurable activities increase the chance of loneliness and depression. Many people find that once they quit gambling, there is a void in their lives. In fact, simple boredom is a common reason for people to gamble.

Think of your life as a jar, which has been filled up with gambling. And then you decide to remove gambling from your life and empty the jar. What you are left with may be an empty or half-empty jar, an empty or half-empty life. This sounds frightening and it may well be. Yet, it is also an opportunity to fill up the jar again with something else, which is not gambling. It is worth investing time and energy in working out how you would like your life to look in the future. The task is to work out how you can end up with a fulfilling and rewarding life, where gambling no longer has a place.

Filling Up the Jar: Striving for Balance

A gambling-free life does not have to mean a non-busy life. In fact, many people fill in their time doing things that are not rewarding but that just have to be done – the 'shoulds' in life. Grocery shopping, cleaning the kitchen floor, picking up the kids from school; they all have to be done, but may not be that satisfying in themselves. Overloading yourself with 'shoulds' will eventually make you feel resentful and grumpy.

This is why it is essential that you include in your gambling-free life a variety of activities, including enjoyable ones – the 'wants'. Chapter 6 on rewards may have already given you a taste of this. If you do not include things that offer pleasure, the gambling will still, in your mind, be the only way you know to enjoy life. Often people say that they cannot afford to do this as they are paying back their debts. However, leading an unhappy life without gambling can cause lapses. It is important to budget for some enjoyable activities in order to make this less likely.

Take a Minute to Think

What will the balance between 'wants' and 'shoulds' be in your life, when gambling is out of the picture?

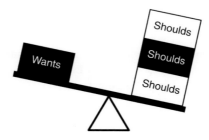

Then, it's also about including social activities, which provide us with a sense of connection to others. Indeed, a key feature of a meaningful life is to have a balance of activities that are fun and pleasurable, activities that give you a sense of achievement, and activities that make you feel connected with others. Pleasurable activities are enjoyable, relaxing, and distracting, but then if you do them in excess, they damage your self-respect. Including activities that provide opportunities for personal achievement will make you feel that you accomplish things and view yourself in a positive light. Social activities will beat loneliness and give you a sense of belonging. Schedule activities which give you a **healthy balance** of:

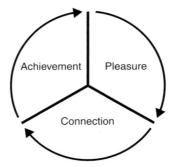

The Gambling-free Life

Thus, you need to be working on developing a range of activities to replace the time spent gambling and thinking about gambling. Not all of these need to be significant or time-consuming activities. The important thing is to have as many different things in your life as possible. A full activities schedule might include such things as work, sports, meeting friends, playing computer games, reading biographies, watching films, cooking, planting vegetables, meals out with a partner or friend, visiting places – it is the variety and range that will stave off boredom and prevent gambling from re-appearing. Your task will be to move from no-man's land to a meaningful, gambling-free life with a variety of activities.

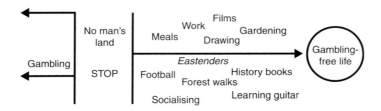

Now, have a look at the list of pleasant activities and try to identify activities that you once enjoyed or that you might consider trying (see '**Pleasant Events/Activities Form**'). Some of these activities require planning, while others are spontaneous. Make sure you select a mixture of both.

Then, we'd urge you to select three activities to try out in the coming week, paying particular attention to having something planned at times when you are more likely to gamble (e.g. weekends, pay day). This offers a way of dealing with cravings and triggers (see Chapters 7 and 8). You may decide to go for a walk in the countryside or take your family on a mini-vacation at the weekend, when you are perhaps most likely to want to gamble.

Finally, be prepared to have to overcome potential obstacles to completion of these activities. Be honest with yourself! To help, we have made a list of the most common obstacles and have discussed how they applied to Ben's case.

Ben's Story

Ben has been abstinent from gambling for three weeks after having gambled problematically for over ten years. Being married with two young kids and in full-time employment, he originally felt that there was no space left for bringing new pleasurable activities into his life. This was due to a long list of 'shoulds' in his week and his guilt for the hardships that his gambling had put his family through. However, he soon realised that going through the motions of living only made gambling seem more appealing. He thus had to find a way around the above obstacles.

- **Commitment:** Putting a new activity plan into action requires strong commitment. Are you willing to change priorities and perhaps also rearrange activities in your life? You may want to have another brief look at Chapter 3 on building motivation. You will certainly need plenty of motivation to change your day-to-day lifestyle.

  Ben found that spending time with his oldest son brought joy to both. Therefore, he made a commitment to take his son to his basketball class a couple of evenings per week.

- **Balance:** Guilt over gambling may stop you from granting permission to yourself to schedule enjoyable or social activities, forcing you to fill up the jar with 'shoulds'. A life overloaded with 'shoulds' places you at greater risk of lapses, so think twice.

  Ben taking his son to his class gave him a sense of pleasure and connection as well as a sense of contributing to his family. This eased his guilt about meeting a friend every couple of weeks.

- **Planning:** Can you anticipate problems or circumstances that could interfere with completing the activities you have planned? Now, can you find a way around them?

  When Ben had to take extra work and could not take his son to his basketball class, he would schedule a fun activity for the two of them or the entire family at the weekend.

- **Enjoyment:** You might discover that the pleasant activities aren't as enjoyable as you had first anticipated. Remember, you are re-training your brain to start enjoying ordinary things, so for now you may just need to persevere with planned activities, even if they don't immediately bring high volumes of joy. Try them for a couple of weeks before switching to something else.

  Spending time with his son did not have the exact same effect as gambling did for Ben but he grew to enjoy it. He also started experiencing a sense of gratitude that he had never felt.

Pleasant Events/Activities Form

Check off any item that you have enjoyed in the past or that you might enjoy now.

- ☐ Being in the country
- ☐ Meeting new people
- ☐ Playing football
- ☐ Going to the beach
- ☐ Rock climbing or mountaineering
- ☐ Playing golf
- ☐ Going to a sports event
- ☐ Reading stories, novels, poems
- ☐ Playing musical instruments
- ☐ Camping
- ☐ Solving puzzles
- ☐ Having lunch with a friend
- ☐ Taking a relaxing hot shower
- ☐ Writing short stories, a novel
- ☐ Exploring, hiking, caving
- ☐ Singing in a group
- ☐ Going to social club meetings
- ☐ Skiing
- ☐ Being with friends
- ☐ Playing pool or billiards
- ☐ Being with your children
- ☐ Bowling
- ☐ Dancing
- ☐ Sitting in the sun
- ☐ Just sitting and thinking
- ☐ Talking about philosophy/religion
- ☐ Playing in a sports competition
- ☐ Going on an outing to the park
- ☐ Having a BBQ
- ☐ Gathering objects (shells, flowers)
- ☐ Being in the mountains
- ☐ Eating a good meal
- ☐ Wrestling or boxing
- ☐ Going to a museum/exhibition
- ☐ Going to the gym
- ☐ Horse riding
- ☐ Going to the movies
- ☐ Coaching someone
- ☐ Meditating
- ☐ Playing board games
- ☐ Swimming
- ☐ Listening to music
- ☐ Crocheting
- ☐ Going to the library
- ☐ Cycling
- ☐ Caring for houseplants
- ☐ Skydiving
- ☐ Driving a sports car
- ☐ Motocross

- ☐ Talking about sports
- ☐ Going to a rock concert
- ☐ Planning a trip or a holiday
- ☐ Doing art or crafts
- ☐ Reading the newspaper
- ☐ Re-arranging or re-decorating a room
- ☐ Reading DIY books
- ☐ Going to a lecture
- ☐ Boating, sailing, canoeing
- ☐ Working in local politics
- ☐ Doing crosswords
- ☐ Playing tennis
- ☐ Woodwork, carpentry
- ☐ Writing a play
- ☐ Having a frank and open conversation
- ☐ Going to church functions
- ☐ Going to business meetings/seminars
- ☐ Acting
- ☐ Window shopping
- ☐ Playing chess
- ☐ Visiting people who are sick
- ☐ Gardening
- ☐ Going to a dance class
- ☐ Riding a motorcycle
- ☐ Going to a fair or carnival
- ☐ Having friends visit
- ☐ Getting a massage
- ☐ Going on a picnic
- ☐ Photography
- ☐ Helping someone
- ☐ Meeting new people
- ☐ Preparing your favourite meal
- ☐ Walking the dog
- ☐ Going to a health club
- ☐ Being with your family
- ☐ Talking on the phone
- ☐ Cooking a cake
- ☐ Keeping a diary
- ☐ Doing yoga
- ☐ Reading a magazine
- ☐ Running, jogging
- ☐ Knitting
- ☐ Needlework
- ☐ People watching
- ☐ Writing letters, cards, notes
- ☐ Taking a walk
- ☐ Scuba diving
- ☐ Mountain climbing
- ☐ Parachuting

My Top Ten favourite activities:

1. _____
2. _____
3. _____
4. _____
5. _____
6. _____
7. _____
8. _____
9. _____
10. _____

Some of these activities can be done on the spur of the moment, while others are better as planned activities. List some from each category:

Spontaneous   **Planned**

_____   _____

_____   _____

_____   _____

_____   _____

Substitute Situations That Trigger Your Desire for Gambling with Pleasant Activities
Having fun will also help you to get through high-risk situations. Here are some specific high-risk times and pleasant alternatives that can be done instead of gambling.

Instead of this   **Try this!**
High-risk time for gambling   Pleasant activity

_____   _____

_____   _____

_____   _____

_____   _____

_____   _____

Whenever you encounter a high-risk situation in the upcoming weeks, **plan to do a pleasant activity instead!**

Adapted from: Petry, N. (2004). Pathological gambling: Etiology, comorbidity and treatment. Washington: American Psychological Association

Skills Practice

1. Review your lifestyle by re-examining the balance between pleasure, achievement, and connection.

2. Look at a copy of the pleasant activities list ('**Pleasant Events/Activities Form**') and pick your favourite activities.

3. Make the commitment to introduce three new activities into your week.

4. Be prepared to overcome barriers by persevering, getting the balance right, planning ahead, and having realistic expectations.

Takeaway Points for Affected Significant Others

1. For a successful recovery, individuals affected by a gambling problem often need to make drastic changes to their entire lifestyle.

2. This may involve increasing pleasurable and social activities to balance them out with things they 'should' do in life.

3. This is to help them overcome the void that quitting gambling leaves behind and improve their mood.

4. Help them identify such activities and join them when appropriate.

10 The Thinking Traps Driving Gambling

Venetia Leonidaki

Most of the time, you are probably aware that gambling is not the solution to your problems. Yet, you may still have thoughts popping into your mind that make you believe the opposite. Your thoughts may sound something like: 'This time will be different' or 'If l win, I will pay my debts and walk away'. This chapter is about being able to catch these thoughts and take some distance from them, before you learn how to challenge them in Chapter 11.

Our Emotional Brain

Humans think all day long. It has been estimated that an average person has around 4,000 thoughts every day! A lot of the time, we are not even aware that we have thoughts popping into our mind. For example, if I asked you to find the way to a street that you had never visited before, you would need to think about this consciously. But if I asked you to cross the road, you would probably not be aware of thinking at all. Both actions involve complex thinking processes, but the latter requires less conscious ones, as crossing the road usually feels automatic. As a result, it takes a fair bit of training and regular practice to be able to catch your thoughts, as some of them are so automatic that you do not even notice them.

Thoughts can be heavily affected by our emotions. For example, when people experience strong emotions, such as feeling frightened or ecstatic, their emotions activate parts of the brain that are not very good at reasoning. This is by no means unique to gambling. Think of Peter, a chap who is deeply in love with his new partner and feels jealous and hurt when the waiter initiates a friendly, but innocent, chat with his sweetheart. Peter finds himself thinking: 'How dare he; I will show him'. Let's also consider Tim, who is afraid of planes and is filled with fear every time minor turbulence happens, thinking 'The plane is falling, I will die'.

In both scenarios, thinking becomes emotional and less rational. This means that our thinking becomes narrow, and it can even lead us into behaving in ways that don't help us in the long-term. Imagine loved-up Peter starting a fight with the waiter or nervous Tim cancelling an important trip because minor turbulence is expected on his flight. In a nutshell, when we feel emotional, our thoughts can often be *irrational or simply unhelpful*. Realising that some thoughts are unhelpful is an important step. We refer to these thoughts here as 'thinking traps', as they can trick us into believing something that is not true. We will soon look at thinking traps specific to gambling, but let's see first how gambling-related thoughts can affect your behaviour.

How Do Thoughts Interact with Emotions, Body, and Behaviours?

Our emotional state can affect our thinking, but the opposite is also true: our thoughts can affect how we feel. Our body and behaviours also interact with thoughts and emotions. Our body captures the physiology that underpins thoughts, emotions, and behaviours. For example, when loved-up Peter felt angry, his body responded with increased heart rate, tension in muscles, tight chest, stomach churning, and feeling hot. Our behaviour is about what we do and often what others could see, if they were observing us. Peter, for example, may have behaved by picking a fight with the waiter or by quietly withdrawing and interacting less with his girlfriend. In fact, in CBT, we can break down all our experience into the following four areas.

Thoughts, Emotions, Body, and Behaviours

These four areas help us to see how people react in helpful and unhelpful ways. They function as part of a system and interact with each other. The system is usually set off by a trigger, which could be something in our environment (e.g. a waiter chatting with a girlfriend, turbulence). The trigger could also be a thought (Peter remembering about someone flirting intensely with an ex-girlfriend) or a feeling or a sensation within our body (Tim feeling dizzy during flight). This system is represented in the form of a 'diamond' shape, as shown in the next diagram. Looking at the diagram, take a moment to think:

- How does the four-area system apply to Peter's and Tim's situation?

By now, you may have also realised that thoughts have a detrimental role in this system, which is the reason for making them the focus here. Thoughts are about the meaning that we give to a situation. The idea here is that if you can catch your thoughts and challenge them, you can also give a new meaning to a situation. This will then affect how you feel about something, how your body feels, and what you end up doing next. Gambling is not an exception to this, as explained next.

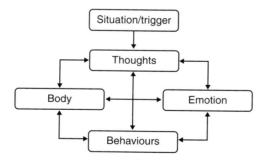

Figure 10.1 Four-areas system.

Tracy's and Alicia's Stories

Both Tracy and Alicia have a history of a gambling problem, with their preferred form of gambling being slot machines. However, Alicia has recently been able to break free from it. They are both faced with the same situation: walking past a pub where there are slot machines. Let's see what happens next:

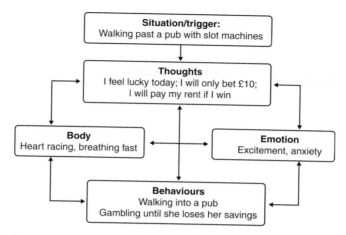

Figure 10. 2 Tracey's four-areas system.

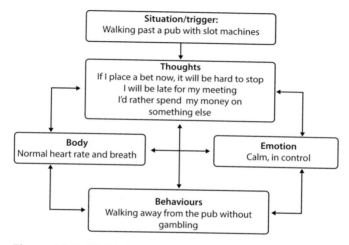

Figure 10.3 Alicia's four-areas system.

- What do you make of Tracey's and Alicia's examples?

Both women were faced with the same situation. Yet, their thoughts were different, which resulted in different emotions, bodily sensations, and, of course, behaviours. Tracey walked in the pub, gambled, and lost her savings, while Alicia walked away. So, your thoughts when you are faced with a gambling-related trigger can make a big difference to how you respond. Now, as you understand better the role of thoughts in your life, you could start breaking down your gambling-related experiences into these four areas: thoughts, emotions, body, and behaviours. So, when you are faced with a trigger (as triggers are defined in Chapter 8), use the four-areas model found in '**Your Four-areas System**' to break down your experience.

As is the case with all skills presented in this book, you need to practise them regularly before they become second nature. Don't worry if you cannot slow yourself down and catch your thoughts in the heat of the moment. In fact, this would be too much to expect from yourself right now.

Take a Minute to Think

You may need to think *back* to a recent situation/trigger and then take time to break it down. It may have been a situation where you thought to gamble but you did not, or a situation where you gave in to your urge to gamble. Either way, it's worth capturing your experience using the four areas. Catching your thoughts can take more practice than the other areas. For now, keep practising asking yourself the following question in any gambling-related situation:

What is going through my mind?

The following sections aim to help you recognise further gambling-related thoughts, including thinking traps.

Catching Your Gambling-permissive Thoughts

Gambling-permissive thoughts are thoughts that act as excuses, giving you permission to gamble, while rationally you know that this is not the wise thing to do. If they go undetected, they affect how you feel inside, how your body feels, and what you end up doing, without you even realising their effect. In fact, you could find yourself gambling without knowing how you found yourself in this situation in the first place. Do you recall this ever having happened to you? Catching these thoughts early will hopefully make you less prone to gambling impulsively. To do this, you first need to be able to recognise them.

Earlier, I mentioned Tracey, whose thoughts led her to walk into the pub and bet on slot machines. Here, we will also look at what happened to Tracey's thoughts before, during, and after gambling.

Prior to Gambling
Thoughts about the outcome of gambling or your ability to control it are examples of gambling-permissive thoughts. While possible, these outcomes may be biased in favour of potential positive consequences of gambling, while your perception of your ability to control gambling is not always an accurate reflection of reality.

Tracey's:	
Thoughts:	'I need to pay my rent; maybe I could turn this £10 into a bit more'
	'Things will be different, I'm in control now'
Emotions:	Stress, excitement, anticipation
Physiology:	Palpitations, feeling hot
Behaviour:	Betting on slot machines

Your Four-areas System

- Practise by breaking down gambling-related experiences into four areas.
- Think of a recent situation where you were reminded of gambling, you gambled, or you had an urge to gamble even if you did not give in.
- To catch your thoughts, ask yourself: What went through my mind at the time?

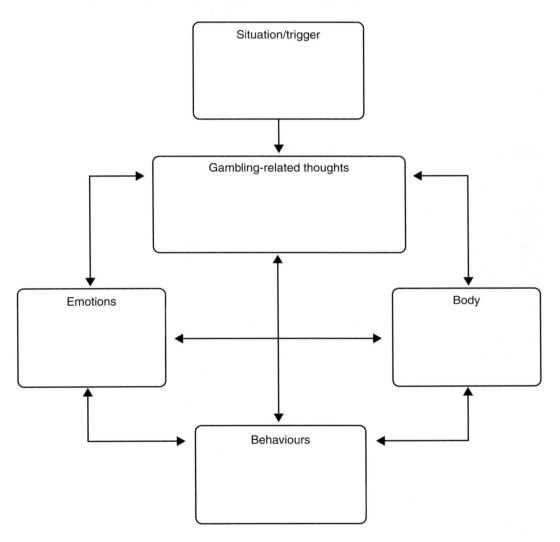

Thoughts about the process of gambling will often act to prolong the gambling episode. These thoughts were so convincing that gambling continued, in spite of Tracey seeing her losses increase.

Tracey's:	'I have been playing on the machine for a while: The jackpot is approaching'
Thoughts:	'I have to get back that money. I'll just get the £10 back, then I'll stop'
	'If I just keep playing for a few more minutes, it will pay out'
Emotions:	Anxiety, worry, hope
Physiology:	Stomach churning, heart racing
Behaviour:	Chasing losses, placing bigger bets

After Gambling
Following gambling, both losses and wins can distort thoughts further in favour of gambling. These eventually lead to a return to gambling and the continuation of the cycle. Tracey's thoughts could have followed either direction, depending on whether she had won or lost.

Tracey's:	'I have to get the money I lost back before anyone finds out'
Thoughts:	'I'll borrow some money from work; tomorrow will be different'
Emotions:	Panic, fear
Physiology:	Sweating, headaches
Behaviour:	Borrowing money, stealing, chasing losses

Or:

Thoughts:	'Jackpot! I knew I could win if I tried hard enough'
	'Easy money' 'It's my lucky day'
Emotions:	Excitement
Physiology:	Tense muscles, heart beating fast
Behaviour:	Returning to gamble another time, chasing wins

'**Examples of Gambling-permissive Thoughts**' aims to help you further by providing a list of typical gambling-permissive thoughts. Take a few minutes to go through it and identify your typical thoughts. As you may have gathered by now, these thoughts distort reality. The same is true for thinking traps, as discussed below.

Common Gambling-related Thinking Traps
This section is about the most common thinking traps underpinning gambling. These are well-researched patterns of biased thinking, leading to unrealistic conclusions about gambling. These thinking traps are not unique to gambling. In fact, as we are going to see, they are universal and apply in various areas in life. However, gambling offers them a fertile habitat where they can flourish. Let us have a look at some examples. Try to identify which thinking traps you most commonly fall into and make a note of them.

Examples of Gambling-permissive Thoughts

Below, there are examples of thoughts that act as excuses, fuelling your gambling habit and making it hard to quit. Can you go through the list to find which of these thoughts pop into your mind most often? Then, next time you catch any of them going through your mind, notice them for what they are: gambling-permissive thoughts, distorting reality.

I will feel happier if I place a bet.

I can't function without gambling.

I have lost several times now, so a big win must be on its way.

It will be a waste of my skills and knowledge if I stop gambling.

I have such a terrible time in my life. Gambling will make things seem better.

I will never be able to quit gambling, so there's no point in trying.

I came across number five twice in the last hour. That is a sign, I can't waste it.

My losses have helped me learn things that will support me to win later.

It was just bad luck and bad circumstances that led me to lose this time.

Gambling will make my future brighter.

My desire to gamble is so overpowering. I can't think of anything else.

Bringing my lucky object will increase my chances of winning.

I won before so it will happen again soon.

I've had a stressful day – gambling will take away my tension.

I feel lucky today – I should place a bet.

I won a fortune before, so it will happen again.

I will never be able to stop gambling.

I have a system in mind that will lead me to win.

If I keep the same numbers every time, sooner or later I will win.

I was so close to winning the jackpot last time – next time I will certainly win.

If I win £100 to pay my bills, I will take the money and leave.

I will bet no more than £20.

Adapted from: Raylu, N., & Oei, T. P. S. (2004). The Gambling Related Cognitions Scale (GRCS): development, confirmatory factor validation and psychometric properties. Addiction, 99, 757.

Gambler's fallacy: Let's start with a quiz, shall we?

Question 1: If I am going to flip a coin ten times in a row, which sequence is most likely to happen?

Sequence A: Ten heads

Sequence B: Five heads and five tails

Question 2: In the national lottery, which sequence is most likely to have the winning numbers?

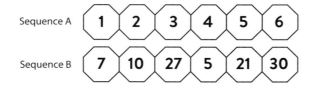

Sequence A:
Sequence B:

You may be wondering what the above quiz has to do with anything. Well, the gambler's fallacy is about our apparent *perception* of odds and probability as compared to the *reality* of probability.

Most people will answer that sequence A is less probable to happen than Sequence B in both situations.

This is because our mind holds the belief that chance will even itself out. However, the correct answers are that both sequences A and B are equally probable to happen on both occasions. Each coin toss is a separate event and carries a 50% chance of either heads or tails. Equally, each number when drawn in the UK lottery is an independent random event with forty-nine possible outcomes. Yet, we tend to believe that we can predict the outcome of a random event based on previous outcomes, which is simply not true.

In a similar way, roulette spins are never 'due' to a particular number or colour. Each run on the wheel is independent from the last. Twenty 'blacks' in a row are as equally likely to be followed by another 'black' as by a 'red'. In fact, this thinking trap took its name after a night in a casino in Monte Carlo in 1913, when the roulette ball fell in black 26 times in a row, resulting in gamblers losing millions of francs betting against black. Much of gambling works by making people think they can predict what will happen when the actual likelihood is far less probable.

The gambler's fallacy is however not unique to gambling. Do you remember Tim, the nervous flyer, from earlier in this chapter? When Tim was deciding whether to book a flight, he was checking the record of airplane crashes in the last three months. This sounds like an odd thing to do, right? Tim thought that given that plane crashes are rare, if one had happened soon before his flight, then it would be less probable for his flight to crash. This of course was not true, but it was Tim falling into a gambler's fallacy mental trap. Indeed, research has found that gambler's fallacy affects how judges make decisions in a court or how loan officers process loan applications.

Illusion of control: The next question may seem beside the point, but remember we are looking at thinking traps that are universal to human thinking.

How would primitive societies try to control weather?

And another random question:

Why did Tim, our nervous flyer, take his lucky stone whenever he would board a plane?

You may be wondering how the above are relevant to your gambling problem? Well, they are. As you most probably have heard, early humans danced to appease mysterious nature forces and bring rain. And as you can guess, Tim was hoping that his stone would bring him good luck and result in a smooth flight. In both situations, the mental trap of illusion of control was operating, resulting in early humans and Tim overestimating their ability to predict and influence outcomes, especially in uncertain situations, nurturing the impression that someone's skills and decisions could make a difference.

When it comes to illusion of control and gambling, consider how some gamblers throw the dice harder or softer to achieve higher or lower numbers, or apply specific techniques to beat the system of FOBT machines. Here are a few examples of how the illusion of control can apply to different types of gambling:

Roulette:	'If I just bet on even reds, I'll definitely win that way'
Sports betting:	'This system is bound to pay off, if I focus on my selections'
Fruits:	'Near miss again! This machine must be fixed. I'll try that one instead'

Attribution bias: Some gamblers tend to attribute their losses externally, for example to bad luck or sabotage, yet explain wins as a result of great personal skill and masterful play. This attribution bias acts to strengthen the illusion of control and causes more gambling.

'I chose all numbers except 0, yet it lands on 0. It has to be fixed'
'I'm just down on my luck, I know the form and I know this one will win'
'I could be professional with this system'

Memory bias: This thinking trap is about how we are more likely to remember one type of memory than another. When it comes to gambling, many people will have an image of a large win in their memory and will use this as 'evidence' that they can make money. On the other hand, they will remember their losses less clearly, being left with the false impression that they are more likely to win than lose. As discussed in Chapter 3, where this thinking trap was first mentioned, a memory aid, such as a cue card, could help you remember both sides of the picture.

'I can make money through gambling': Unlike the previous thinking traps that are universal and apply to various areas in life beyond gambling, this one is specific to gambling and your expectations about the outcome of your gambling. Chapter 11 gives you more information about one's expectations about gambling, what they are like, and how to deal with them, but here we focus on a particular expectation that we so commonly witness in individuals seeking help in our clinic and which fuels their motivation for gambling.

One of the most important beliefs that must change when trying to stop gambling is that you can make money from gambling. This is different from winning: anyone can win at gambling, if they play for long enough. *But can you make money from it?* Some people have started out gambling as a means of providing income, and we are often told of instances where people have made money out of gambling. But I want you to revisit the question just posed with a little emphasis: *can* you *make money from gambling?*

This is a different question to whether someone can make money from gambling. There are ways of being more successful when gambling, but making money takes certain skills, strategies, and techniques. It may even require a certain temperament. In Chapter 2, we looked at the different types of gambling that exist. Here, we want to revisit them:

1. Social	Type:	Grand National, lottery, cards at Christmas
	This individual may not particularly enjoy gambling but will gamble once in a while as part of social norms.	
2. Recreational	Type:	Bookmakers, casino, online, poker
	Recreational gambling takes up a proportion of one's weekly time. Individuals might spend a significant proportion of their wages on gambling or view it as an activity and interest and a form of entertainment.	
3. Professional	Type:	Sporting events, spread betting, card games
	This category is also termed 'business' gambling. Individuals in this group use betting to make money and most often will not necessarily enjoy gambling or engage in other gambling activities. Risks are minimised. The professional/business gambler will have strict rules about not chasing losses or wins.	
4. Compulsive	Type:	Any gambling activity
	Compulsive gambling is set apart from all other types because of problems with control and limits. Individuals gamble compulsively, chasing losses and wins. They find themselves unable to leave a game/bet when in a positive, winning position. They spend more time gambling and lose more as a result.	

Take a Minute to Think

Do your view your gambling as social, recreational, professional, or compulsive?

The chances are that if you are reading this book, your gambling is compulsive and you find it hard to control it.

Which of the above four types of gambling is more likely to result in making money?

Our guess is professional, followed by recreational gambling.

Compulsive gambling is not likely to help you make money; because it's emotionally driven, setting limits is difficult – almost impossible – and chasing losses is part and parcel of it.

If your gambling is compulsive, then you are not very good at gambling, you may be predisposed to compulsive behaviours, and it's highly unlikely that you will make money from it. There will be plenty of other things that you can do well, but it may be time to accept that gambling is not one of them.

The list of gambling-permissive thoughts and thinking traps that we have considered so far is not exhaustive but describes processes found at the heart of gambling. In order to identify these thoughts popping into your head, it may be helpful to think about a recent gambling episode and try to remember what was going through your mind at the time. You could then write your thoughts down in the 'Thought Diary', alongside the other three areas of the four-areas system introduced earlier.

You may have found the content of this chapter challenging to read at times. This may be because we touch upon and challenge beliefs that are found at the heart of gambling. The purpose of this chapter is to spell out any unhelpful beliefs that drive your gambling, as this is the best way to make them less automatic, more conscious, and help you to take a step back from them and start questioning them. We appreciate that doing this may not feel easy or even enjoyable for you. Yet, if this chapter has made you feel uneasy, perhaps this is because something inside you is shifting. Remember, change is taking us out of our comfort zone, so feeling uncomfortable when reading this chapter may be a great sign of change. The next chapter focuses explicitly on how to challenge thoughts that fuel your gambling. Ready? Take a deep breath and carry on reading.

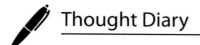

Thought Diary

Catching gambling-related thoughts, emotions, bodily sensations, and behaviours

Situation/ trigger	Gambling-related thoughts	Emotions	Body sensations	Behaviours
What was happening, where were you? Any reminders of gambling around you?	*What went through your mind? Did you catch a gambling-permissive thought? Did you spot a mental trap?*	*What emotions did you feel? e.g. anxiety, excitement*	*What was happening in your body? e.g. heart racing, feeling tense*	*What did you do? Did you give in to the urge? Did you resist? Did you do something else?*

Skills Practice

- Practise breaking your gambling down into thoughts, emotions, body sensations, and behaviours. This will help you see how each area affects another and the key role that thoughts play in your gambling.

- Gambling-permissive thoughts act as excuses that fuel gambling, so practise catching them and writing them down in order to create some space from them.

- Gambling provides a fertile environment for thinking traps affecting our judgement and memory. Start recognising them so you don't fall into them.

Takeaway Points for Affected Significant Others

- We all have an emotional brain and our thinking often becomes irrational when we experience strong emotions. This also happens in gambling.

- Gambling provides a natural habitat for thinking traps that distort our judgement and memory universally.

- This chapter helps gamblers to start recognising irrational thoughts and take a step back from them by breaking down their experience.

- This skill requires a lot of practice and it is particularly hard to apply in the heat of the moment, especially early on.

11 Challenging Gambling Thinking and Beliefs

Frank Ryan

In the previous chapter, you learnt how gambling affects our thinking and how to be more alert to gambling-permissive thoughts and your thinking falling into mental traps. In this chapter you will first learn to re-evaluate these thoughts and replace them with thinking more likely to sustain change in the long term. Second, you will be introduced to three coping strategies to enable you to think your way out of situations when you are at risk of gambling.

Your Expectations about Gambling

When you decide to place a bet, it's usually because you expect that the outcome will be good, whether it's anticipating a win or that gambling will just make you feel better. As mentioned in Chapter 6, there is a very strong loop in your brain that tells you gambling is good, reinforced by the times where you have won or enjoyed yourself by gambling.

Our expectations are usually based on recollections of our prior experience, but as your learnt in Chapter 10, our thinking is affected by memory bias, which is especially true when it comes to gambling. In other words, your brain is really good at remembering positive memories related to gambling, such as recalling the joy of an unexpected win or the feeling that your worries seemed to vanish when you were immersed in gambling.

But what if you didn't think you had a realistic chance of winning, or you didn't think gambling would make you feel better? Would you be so eager to place a bet or put a coin in a machine? If you really held the above expectations, you would think again and make a different choice. This is a key theme of this chapter: re-evaluating your beliefs about the consequences of gambling. This re-appraisal of your beliefs will enable you to make more rational decisions and sustain the changes you want to make in managing your gambling.

Craig's Story

Craig sought support to manage his difficulty controlling his online gambling. When Craig saw a gambling advert on TV, these thoughts flashed through his mind:

- *'I can win at this; I'm good at poker'*
- *'Playing will make me feel better, I'll forget about my problems'.*
- *'I'll stop being bored, I'll get a buzz from playing'.*

You may be able to tell that Craig is having gambling-permissive thoughts, which you read about in the previous chapter. In fact, it's a particular type of gambling-permissive thought, focusing on his expectations about the outcome of gambling. These predictions about what would happen if he was to gamble seemed plausible to Craig. His predictions have been at least partly true on some occasions. But his predictions are also one-sided, which Craig realises when he starts reflecting upon them.

On a scale from 0 to 100%, Craig initially believed his thoughts 90% of the time. He had often won at poker in the past; he was rarely bored when playing and found that he could forget about a traumatic experience he had five years earlier.

When he reflected more on his gambling history, Craig recollected memories connected to the smaller loop: gambling is bad. As he started entertaining another side to the story, his expectations about gambling changed to the following:

- *'I mostly lose in the end'*
- *'I will feel ashamed and guilty when my family finds out'.*
- *'I will feel really down after a gambling session'.*

Craig found himself believing less and less in his original gambling-permissive thoughts (I can win this – rate of belief: 50%) and started embracing more strongly the above expectations (70%), making gambling a less attractive option.

The above applies equally to you in your quest to move away from your gambling problem. Accordingly, in order to overcome your gambling issues, it is important that you:

1. Identify your own expectations about gambling.
2. Estimate the strength and/or evaluate the truth of this expectation.
3. Develop an alternative, more balanced expectation.

Take a Minute to Think

To help you get started, it is useful to identify your expectations about gambling. Do you have expectations of:

- Winning?
- Making money?
- Feeling happier, less bored, stressed?
- Exhilaration or excitement?
- Positive social interactions; being part of a group?
- Being your own person, making your own choices?

If you do, then make a note of your expectations and focus more closely on them in the exercise found in '**How to Catch and Evaluate Your Expectations about Gambling**'. This is about how to evaluate your thoughts and practise developing new beliefs which capture the full picture and not only one side of it.

Please note that although we focus on your expectations about gambling and beliefs about beliefs in the next two exercises, the same skill of identifying an expectation or a thought, rating it, and developing an alternative perspective could apply to other types of gambling-permissive thoughts, found in '**How to Catch and Evaluate Your (Meta)Beliefs about Gambling**'.

How to Catch and Evaluate Your Expectations about Gambling

Catching and evaluating gambling-related expectations: an example					
Gambling-related expectation	Rating (0 = never true, 100 = always true)	Evidence for	Evidence against	Alternative belief after evaluation	Re-rating (0 = never true, 100 = always true)
What will happen if I gamble?	*How true is my belief?*	*What makes you think this is true?*	*What makes you think this is not true?*	*What belief captures the full picture?*	*How true is your new belief?*
I will feel happier when I log on and start betting	70%	I have spent hours gambling online and really enjoyed it	When I reached my credit card limit and had to tell my partner I had been betting	I will feel happier for a while but I usually feel unhappy afterwards	70%

Catching and weighing gambling-related expectations					
Gambling-related expectation	Rating (0 = never true, 100 = always true)	Evidence for	Evidence against	Alternative belief after evaluation	Re-rating (0 = never true, 100 = always true)
What will happen if I gamble?	*How true is my belief?*	*What makes you think this is true?*	*What makes you think this is not true?*	*What belief captures the full picture?*	*How true is your new belief?*

Using the example as a starting point, fill in the rest of the worksheet by recalling or imagining a situation where you gambled or thought to do so.

How true were the expectations about gambling in the heat of the moment and when compared to the actual outcome?

Recalling the example in the worksheet above, can you come up with a new belief that brings together the two sides of the coin (what is true and what is not true about your original expectation)?

When you next find yourself thinking about gambling, aim to make your predictions or expectations of the outcome more in line with what is actually likely to happen.

If I gamble, the outcome will be	How true is this belief, when 0 = never true, 100 = always true	What makes you think this is true?	When has this not been true?	Re - Rate how true the belief is now, using 0–100 scale	Alternative belief, following evaluation.
Example: I will feel happier when I log on and start betting	70%	I have spent hours gambling online and really enjoyed it	When I reached my credit card limit and had to tell my partner I had been betting	30%	I will feel happier for a while but usually feel unhappy afterwards

Beliefs about Beliefs

This is not a misprint! The way you view your own gambling-related thoughts can determine whether or not you choose to gamble again. Expectations, mentioned above, are specific to a particular occasion e.g. *'I'm on a lucky streak so I will place a winning bet'*. On the other hand, beliefs about beliefs, sometimes called *'meta-beliefs'* or *'meta-cognitions'* are more general. Because these beliefs seem plausible, they can undermine your efforts to overcome your gambling problems. Consider, for example these gambling-related beliefs:

- *'I can't control my thoughts about gambling'*
- *'My thoughts about gambling will continue until I give in to them'*
- *'Thinking about gambling means I will gamble'*
- *'Gambling is the only way to stop me worrying about my job/ relationship/health'*
- *'Thoughts about gambling can overwhelm my willpower'*

Now, pause and reflect for a few moments. Recall a recent time when you were actively engaged in gambling or you were preoccupied with thoughts about gambling. Do you recall having had similar thoughts? Or any other thoughts about your thoughts regarding gambling?

Hopefully you do not feel entirely confused after reading the above. If you do, don't worry.! We deal with meta-beliefs in a similar way to any other thoughts related to gambling. The key is to notice the thought simply as a thought and not an instruction to act on it. It is important to recognise when you are having these thoughts. This enables you to either divert your attention from the thoughts or evaluate the thought or belief by weighing up the evidence for and against the beliefs.

'How to Catch and Evaluate Your (Meta)Beliefs about Gambling' is about catching and challenging these types of thoughts.

How to Catch and Evaluate Your (Meta)Beliefs about Gambling

Catching and evaluating gambling-related expectations: an example					
Gambling-related belief	Rating (0 = never true, 100 = always true)	Evidence for	Evidence against	Alternative belief after evaluation	Re-rating (0 = never true, 100 = always true)
What do you believe about gambling?	*How true is my belief?*	*What makes you think this is true?*	*What makes you think this is not true?*	*What belief captures the full picture?*	*How true is your new belief?*
Thinking about gambling makes me gamble	80%	I have frequently gambled after thinking about it	I have often gambled on impulse without thinking about it; I have thought about gambling and not subsequently gambled	Thinking about gambling increases the likelihood of gambling, but does not cause it. My thoughts are just thoughts, more like a warning signal than a command	60%
Gambling will take my worries away and makes me feel better	95%	I can forget my worries when I am gambling	Sometimes my worries remain. My stress levels often increase after gambling	Gambling can distract me from my worries or stress for a short period but doesn't resolve anything. Gambling adds to my worries and makes me feel bad.	100%

Catching and evaluating gambling-related expectations					
Gambling-related belief	Rating (0 = never true, 100 = always true)	Evidence for	Evidence against	Alternative belief after evaluation	Re-rating (0 = never true, 100 = always true)
What do you believe about gambling?	*How true is my belief?*	*What makes you think this is true?*	*What makes you think this is not true?*	*What belief captures the full picture?*	*How true is your new belief?*

Your thoughts and beliefs about gambling can increase the likelihood of resumed gambling. It is important that you change your relationship with these thoughts and beliefs.

First, simply being aware of these thoughts is important. This can act as an early warning that you need to divert your attention elsewhere, perhaps to focus on the long-term benefits of a life free from gambling, or engaging in one of the valued activities you listed in Chapter 9.

Second, ask yourself: How true or valid these thoughts and beliefs are – where's the evidence? In the above worksheet, try to identify and evaluate your gambling-related thoughts and beliefs by weighing up the evidence for and against. Then write an alternative, more balanced version in the column on the right.

Three Coping Strategies

The key to breaking free from problem gambling is to anticipate when your resolve will be challenged. In this section you will learn three ways to deal with the inevitable challenges. First you will learn to develop a plan that entails a simple coping tactic if you find yourself approaching a gambling opportunity. Second, you will be encouraged to look beyond the immediate consequences of gambling and focus instead on the long- term positive outcomes linked to restraint. Third, you will be introduced to the ancient art of mindfulness. A mindful stance can enable you to detach yourself from urges and cravings and to appreciate the need to be kind to yourself on your recovery journey.

1. Good Intentions Are Not Enough – You Need a Good Plan as Well!

Good intentions are necessary but ultimately insufficient for achieving any important goal. Your intention of breaking free from problem gambling also requires personally tailored plans or coping strategies. These need to be ready in advance of the inevitable 'close encounters' with gambling opportunities. If you find yourself in a 'high-risk' situation you are more likely to avoid gambling if you have a plan.

Remember that a gambling situation can evoke strong feelings which can prevent you thinking in a cool, rational way. That is why preparation is key. But you shouldn't need too many plans, just enough to respond to predictable events, your triggers. The usual format is '*If … Then*' as follows: *If* I am thinking about engaging in gambling on my phone, *then* I will switch it off and go for a walk.

If I have had a stressful day at work, and think I will start betting, *then* I will visit the gym on my way home.

Take a Minute to Think

Now, having looked at the above examples, can you devise your own action plans?

First, think of the triggers and cues that you have identified when working on Chapter 7. For example, if your phone app sends you alerts or offers of free betting, it could be '*If I am offered a free bet, I will switch my phone to "Airplane" mode for 30 minutes*'. Or '*If I am really thinking about logging on to gamble, I will turn on the mindfulness app on my phone*' (see below for more information on mindfulness).

The important point is to have these plans identified and rehearsed *in advance*. If you are confronted with a gambling opportunity, your decision-making and problem-solving can be overwhelmed

List your plans here:

If _____ Then _____

If _____ Then _____

If _____ Then _____

You could also go back to Chapter 7 on coping with craving and urges to remember the skills that you learnt there, as you could make them part of your plan.

2. Consider the Consequences: The 'Now versus Later' Strategy

Given the growth of online gambling opportunities, initiating gambling is literally at your fingertips. This gives you little time to think rationally, or seek support, to prevent a gambling lapse. Your emotional brain will be focused on the immediate attraction of gambling. But you can override this by thinking ahead! This brings your cool rational mind into play and can enable you to arrive at a balanced decision. Look at '"**Now versus Later" Strategy**' below and fill in the blank sections when considering a gambling episode from your past.

3. Mindful Acceptance

The above coping strategies require well-justified effort but can be exhausting if you encounter repeated triggers. What if you haven't enough mental energy or willpower to apply your micro-plans, the '*If, then*' plans formed in advance? Or it seems too difficult to scope the short- and long-term consequences of the '*Now versus Later*' plan? Sometimes, trying to think your way out of a gambling scenario can trigger a rebound effect. (A well-known psychology experiment showed that trying *not* to think of something – in this case images of white bears – leads to a paradoxical increase in intrusive thoughts and images of creatures!) An alternative to grappling with impulsive gambling thoughts is to adopt a detached, mindful stance.

 ## 'Now versus Later' Strategy

Here are some examples contrasting consequences of gambling: immediate and delayed, positive and negative.

Next, recall a time that you gambled or felt tempted to do so. Think about and write down the different consequences.

Practising this skill will help you take a step back to reflect. Simply pausing to reflect – especially about the delayed consequences – can put the brakes on the 'hot' emotional thoughts and help you to choose to remain free from gambling.

	NOW (Immediate Consequences)	LATER (Delayed Consequences)
Positive Outcomes *Example*	*Excitement of anticipated win; stopped feeling stressed about work.*	*I've learned that it is difficult to control my impulse to gamble. I will be able to see the warning signs earlier if this happens again.*
Negative Outcomes *Example*	*I have no spare cash, just using my overdraft. I've let myself down.*	*I've lost more money and I've had to borrow until the end of the month.*
	Now	**Later**
My Positive Outcomes		
My Negative Outcomes		

Mindfulness is a form of meditation that entails paying attention to the present, moment by moment. Typically, your mind wanders, dwelling on the past or zooming ahead into the future. Mindfulness is about simply noticing whatever is going on in your mind and body, without judgement. Mindfulness aims to keep you anchored in the present by enabling you to gently escort your attention back to the here and now in the face of the routine cascade of memories, daydreams, desires, and worries. Mindfulness is not a remedy or cure in itself, but can be a valuable asset in breaking free from any habit or unwanted emotion.

Mindfulness needs to be practised regularly, typically once a day for fifteen to thirty minutes in order for you to experience its considerable benefits. Key techniques for learning and maintaining mindfulness are:

1. *Focusing* and *sustaining* attention, for example on your breathing.
2. *Gently switching* attention away from something distracting (which could be one of your gambling triggers).
3. *Detaching or distancing* yourself from thoughts and feelings, e.g. '*I am just having that thought*', or '*I am just experiencing that emotion*'.

There are many free-to-use apps that you can download to your smart phone to introduce you to the practice of mindfulness. Once downloaded, all you need to do is to set aside time every day where you are able to sit or rest in a quiet space. Teachers of mindfulness use the analogy of a muscle which strengthens with exercise. Similarly, the 'mental muscle' of mindfulness grows with regular practice.

In this chapter, you explored how your beliefs and expectations about gambling and its consequences can influence your decision-making and subsequent behaviour. You were encouraged to develop more realistic expectations about the consequences of gambling in place of the false promises that fostered it. You were introduced to new ways of thinking and planning ahead to cope with gambling impulses. The ancient practice of mindfulness was also described as a means of pausing and reflecting in a noisy and busy world. This is a toolkit that you can select from according to your preferences. Discovering what works best for you in particular situations will take practice. Expect setbacks and be kind to yourself when they happen. In fact, the next chapter is all about how to deal with lapses as well as a full-blown relapse.

Skills Practice

- Identify your expectations of your past gambling. Ask yourself how valid or true these subsequently proved to be. Then develop more realistic beliefs about the short-term and long-term consequences of gambling.

- Anticipate when you will be challenged in your quest to keep free from gambling. Develop simple contingency plans that give you an exit from the triggering situation.

- Discover mindfulness, the art of being in the present, just noticing without judging. Practice this every day.

Takeaway Points for Affected Significant Others

- Compulsive gambling is enabled and maintained by misleading beliefs and false expectations about outcomes and consequences.

- Recognising, challenging, and replacing these thoughts is the key to breaking free from gambling-related harms.

- Anticipate challenges and prepare action plans to manage temptation.

- Reflection and mindfulness are important in maintaining change and building resilience.

12 How to Get Back on Track after a Slip

Annika Lindberg

The idea of relapsing does not sit well with any person undergoing recovery from addiction. Yet a lapse, or even a full relapse, is often part of the recovery journey away from gambling-related harms and the focus of this chapter.

Is Thinking of Relapse a Bit Like Tempting Fate?

When we ask our clients in the clinic to do relapse planning, it first often feels like it contradicts their intention of remaining abstinent. The truth is that you can do both: aim for the best (abstinence) and plan for the worst (relapse). Think of relapse prevention in this chapter as being part of a fire drill. Nobody wants to think about being in a fire. However, a fire escape plan will help you identify which actions to take should the fire alarm warn you that a fire has started.

When initially embarking on their recovery journey, most people often present as optimistic and determined about their future recovery. At times, they even feel 'invincible'. While this mindset may feel helpful, it could also create a barrier and even place you at risk. Talking about how to prevent a lapse is not done with the intention of casting doubt and negativity on your journey ahead. It merely aims to encourage you to remain open and willing to explore how to prevent a lapse from happening or, if one occurs, treat it as a learning experience.

What Is the Difference between a Lapse and a Relapse?

Despite best intentions, things sometimes can go wrong. There is however a major difference between an occasional and/or unintentional lapse, and a full-blown relapse.

Take a Minute to Think

We think of a *lapse* as a one-off slip back to gambling, perhaps by placing one or a few bets in quick concession over a day or so. A *relapse* is a return to old behaviours and habits. It might still be brief but could also become a prolonged episode of gambling that lasts for months or years.

Generally speaking, the longer the gambling is allowed to persist after a lapse, the more difficult it becomes to get back on track. Therefore, *the faster you recognise and manage a lapse, the less likely it is to become a full-blown relapse.* This is not to say that a relapse cannot be managed but it can get considerably tougher and costlier.

We would not focus on relapse so closely if we did not know that it is often part and parcel of the recovery journey.

The table below called 'Common Reasons for a Relapse' summarises the most common reasons for a relapse.

 ## Common Reasons for a Relapse

Take time to have a look and consider which of these reasons are most likely to apply to you.

Most Common Reasons for a Lapse/Relapse
• You fail to add barriers that prevent you from accessing money, gambling sites, and gambling venues.
• You stop practising the skills covered in previous chapters that have helped you get better (rewards for not gambling, coping skills for craving, activity planning, dealing with triggers, catching and challenging thoughts).
• Your gambling has stopped but nothing else has changed. You have neither found other rewarding activities to replace gambling with nor have you changed your routine.
• You develop overconfidence in your recovery process. 'Red flags', such as thoughts or urges (that may indicate a looming lapse) can therefore go unchecked for longer before being detected.
• You have reached a 'plateau' in your recovery where things start feeling comfortable but stagnant; boredom sets in and thoughts of gambling re-emerge.
• Life throws you stressful events and you feel as though you lack the problem-solving skills or the emotional resources to deal with them. Gambling seems to be the only escape.
• Impulsivity 'strikes' and causes a temporary 'shut down' of your rational thinking.

Which of the reasons for lapsing are most likely to apply to you?

_____

_____

_____

_____

_____

_____

_____

_____

_____

_____

_____

_____

Which ones have previously led to a lapse for you?

_____

_____

_____

_____

_____

_____

_____

_____

_____

_____

_____

_____

Although a lapse may often feel sudden, impulsive and out of the blue, there are
almost always warnings signs acting as smoke alarms. These signs can be slight urges

and fleeting thoughts at first, which can be easy to dismiss unless you are paying close attention. Later on, they may be strong cravings and persistent thoughts before they turn into a lapse or even a full-blown relapse.

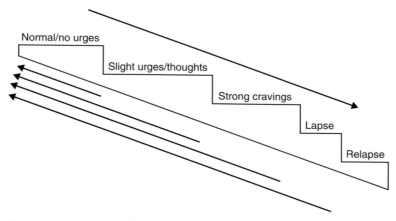

Figure 12.1 Stages of a relapse.

What you may notice in the diagram above, is that the further down you go at the different stages of a relapse, the longer the distance you have to cover to get back to a place where you are free from urges. Thus, the sooner you take action to reverse the direction, the better it will be. The further down the relapse stages, the more difficult it becomes to pull yourself back up.

Compare the two stories below and, using the diagram, think about how these men's responses to a slip end up determining the consequence and endurance of their lapse.

David's Story

David had been abstinent for six months. Having initially spent some months in residential rehab, he had been able to get some time under his belt without having a bet. His family had recently started talking to him after years of having limited contact (due to David's many lies and failed promises). He had also taken some progressive steps to repay his debt. Sadly, he had not started up any new activities or hobbies. Having not worked during his rehab stay, he had decided to focus solely on work once he got out again, as he needed to make some quick money. Work also helped him push away his emotions. Several months had passed by with David not touching up on his acquired skills.

Trigger: One day he had a big argument with his brother and they fell out. David was yet again yearning for his old familiar 'crutch'....

Joe's Story

Joe had attended therapy for four months and had started feeling confident in his recovery. He did not think he would gamble ever again. Having previously made a point of removing direct access to money by leaving his debit card in his office safe, he had gone back to carry his card around in his pocket. He felt that as a 'grown man' it was important to manage his own money. Joe had resumed his old hobby of football. This had turned out to be helpful in keeping fit, busy, and in a good mood. With the end of the summer approaching and the weather getting worse, he had however started to disengage with his team. He was beginning to feel listless and bored. He was also becoming isolated. Thoughts of gambling had re-emerged …

Trigger: His wages arrived into his bank account. Joe experienced cravings and he felt that he could afford to lose £200. He bet £200 and lost it all immediately …

You may now be wondering what happened afterward …

David's Bet

Following on from his lapse, David engaged in extended negative thinking about having failed in his recovery. This, in turn, lead to increased self-loathing, shame, guilt, and despair. He ended up feeling utterly hopeless about his prospect of continued recovery and as if he had blown it all. Having invested in several months of rehab, he could not accept that he had lapsed. Rather than using the tools he still *did* have access to, he focused on how he had 'failed' in his recovery. Consequently, his behaviour gave way to continued gambling, instead of David applying actions that could help it come to a stop. He ended up gambling another year before he decided to give recovery another go.

Joe's Bet

Joe knew that it would be unwise to treat his lapse as a sign that he had made a permanent return to gambling. Instead of engaging in 'all-or-nothing thinking', Joe quickly decided it would be better to cut his losses and ensure he allowed a bit of space to calm down. This enabled him to return to a more rational way of thinking about his lapse. Even if he was initially angry and disappointed with himself, he resolutely decided to analyse and learn from what had just happened. As a result, he took some helpful steps to protect against another set-back (see the 'Behaviour' section in Figure 12.2). He has remained in recovery ever since.

You can see a snapshot of David's and Joe's stories illustrated in Figure 12.2.

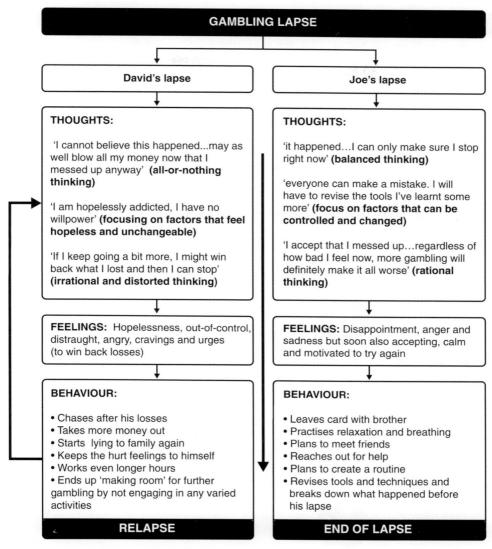

Figure 12.2 Diagram representing lapse aftermaths.

What to Do in Case of a Lapse?

We are going to look closer at how to act in case of a lapse by pretending that you are part of a movie set. So far, the recording has been going to plan, but when the going gets tough it is time to stop the recording for a bit. Think of yourself as the main character in a film about your recovery when something suddenly triggers you to have a lapse. The following section could be used as a metaphor for the steps to take in order to prevent it from turning into a relapse.

1. Press Pause

In case of a lapse, the absolute first thing you need to do is to stop the tape running by pressing the pause button! This step holds true *irrespective* of how you feel or think, and whether you are winning or losing. Granted that any further gambling will only be made possible with a supply of money, it is critically important that *your access to money (and ideally also gambling venues) is immediately disrupted.* Addictive behaviours, such as gambling, 'hijack' the brain very fast, causing autopilot to set in. When you place a bet, your thoughts could easily get distorted and you could find yourself in an impulsive mode, regardless of whether you encounter wins or losses. Putting an immediate stop to the gambling activity by disrupting all routes of access is therefore the most sensible thing you can do.

Think of it a bit like cutting all contact with a partner that has broken up with you. You probably struggle to do it and occasionally you might yearn to reach out. Despite the short-term hurt that would be natural to experience, most people would probably agree that in the longer term, having a clean break makes it easier to accept things as they are and move on with one's life.

2. Rewind and Zoom In

A close-up perspective will help you inspect the details of your lapse. The point here is to take time to break down and deconstruct your recent lapse(s). To apply maximum focus on the detail, we suggest an adapted version of the four-areas system exercise in Chapter 10. '**Analysing a Lapse**' takes you through a recent lapse and helps you break it down in even finer detail, while also elaborating on the short- and long-term consequences. This can be a helpful way of tuning in better to early signs of a lapse, so that you can catch yourself before going off-track in the future.

3. Zoom Out and Press Play

In the second part of this exercise, you need to zoom out, in order to view events from a broader perspective. Consider whether your short-term consequences were worth the long-term consequences (columns 5 and 6 of '**Analysing a Lapse**'). By zooming out and seeing the bigger picture, your image might now hold clues as to what aspects of your recovery have remained unaddressed and help you to find new solutions.

If, for instance, you notice that lapses are happening each time your work/life balance is not attended to, or whenever you stop going for support meetings, then this gives you something tangible to address for the future.

Engaging in self-blame and rumination can be tempting following a lapse, but 'beating yourself up' will only add salt to the wounds and place you at greater risk of gambling again. Important as it is to allow yourself to feel upset and disappointed, it is equally important to accept *that you are going through a difficult journey*. Falling off the wagon could help you learn a lesson to take on board in your journey moving forward, when you press play and let the tape continue to roll. Try to *be kind and forgiving towards yourself*, even when this feels counter-intuitive. This is the best way to prevent a lapse from becoming a full-blown relapse.

Your Anti-relapse Plan

Having now done hard work on understanding lapses, we would like you to take a few minutes to construct your own safety plan. We started this chapter by mentioning that having a well-rehearsed plan for what to do in case of a lapse can make all the difference if one actually occurs. Having a concise anti-relapse plan enables you to quickly rehearse your risk factors and desired responses.

In fact, the more you rehearse your anti-relapse plan, the more natural it will feel to take appropriate action, even during an emotional state. On the flip side, having no plan at all can make it dangerously easy to go down an old familiar spiral again when faced with a lapse.

Just as the gambling behaviour has been reinforced by countless repetitions, it is important that you allow yourself the opportunity to mentally revise and repeat your script of how to take action to prevent a lapse or a relapse.

As a final summary of the learning from this chapter, try to complete '**My Personal Anti-relapse Plan**'. When you are done, make a regular diary appointment with yourself to review and update your plan. You might notice that lifestyle changes and time spent in recovery affects the answers to the questions above, hence this exercise requires review and adaptations from time to time.

Analysing a Lapse

Analysing a lapse and its aftermath

Triggers (could be external such as 'paid from work' or internal such as 'boredom')	Thoughts	Feelings	Gambling-related behaviours (these may precede the gambling)	Immediate positive consequences	Long-term consequences
David: Having an argument with his brother	'I can't cope with this – I will just gamble a bit …'	Anger Stress Urges	Returned to slots	Numbed feelings	Prolonged gambling Money losses Self-loathing Shame Family difficulties
Joe: Inactivity/ boredom Receiving his wages	'I will gamble just a set amount …'	Excitement Cravings	Placed a bet	The feeling of 'rush' and excitement (15 min)	Money losses Stress of lapse Shameful feelings

My Personal Anti-relapse Plan

Here are the main reasons that I don't want to gamble again:	1.
	2.
	3.
These are the things I will do to prevent myself from returning to gambling:	1.
	2.
	3.
Here are some of positive changes I have enjoyed since stopping:	1.
	2.
	3.
If I experience an urge or encounter a high-risk situation, these are the things I will do:	1.
	2.
	3.
If I do lapse, these are the things that I will do to avoid it turning into a relapse:	1.
	2.
	3.

Skills Practice

- The faster you recognise and manage a lapse, the less likely it is to turn into a full-blown relapse.

- Be a step ahead of the game by recognising early the most common reasons that could lead to a lapse.

- If you have a lapse, press pause, rewind and zoom in, and then zoom out and press play so you can continue your recovery journey.

- Create a regular diary appointment with yourself where you go over and adapt your anti-relapse plan. This helps you stay up-to-date with all of your recent learning.

Takeaway Points for Affected Significant Others

- Lapses do unfortunately occur even to the most dedicated individuals. They are part of the recovery journey and can be managed. It does not necessarily mean that your loved one did not want to stay in recovery!

- Many reasons can lead to a lapse and becoming familiar with them here could help you notice early signs that your loved one has missed . This may enable you to act as an additional support.

- If your loved one has had a lapse, it is useful to wait for the emotions to settle down before trying to communicate about what has happened. It may also be important to get personal support for your own feelings from friends, other family members, or a professional.

- Reflecting on the lapse and breaking it down is certainly more helpful than blaming and acting as if all the good work has been ruined. That said, you are entitled to your own reactions and it is understandable if you are feeling betrayed, hurt and disappointed.

- It may be useful if you and your loved one can work together on their anti-relapse plan, as this could help generate more strategies.

13 Don't 'Switch On' the Auto-pilot: Future Planning

Ryan Kemp

At this stage, you will have done quite a lot of work and may have already made plenty of changes. Perhaps things are more manageable and perhaps you have achieved a solid period of not gambling. It would be easy to think that the job is done, but that would be a mistake. Research into how recovery progresses shows that good starts are often undone by complacency and bad luck. Complacency is falling back into bad habits, even if these are not directly gambling related. Bad luck is about events that happen that we were not expecting. The problem with bad luck is it happens to everyone, all the time. Bad luck is just another name for life.

Adverse life events happen to everyone, and these changes can be disruptive, often leading to gambling again. These life events that can trigger gambling can be positive or negative, so realising that both are potentially risky is important. Moving house, a promotion, or a large inheritance can leave you feeling great and perhaps a little 'over-confident'. Life events can also happen to those close to you, and friends and your family may become preoccupied with their own concerns and act differently towards you.

'List of Top Stressful and Exciting Life Circumstances' provides a list of these significant life circumstances. You will notice Christmas and retirement are on the list! It may seem odd to see that some positive experiences are included here, but exciting things can also be stressful because they cause disruption. Any of these life changes has the potential to lead to gambling. Take some time to go through this list and ideally discuss it with someone you trust, so you can identify which of these events are more likely to put you at risk of gambling.

What we see from this example is that Claudine would have benefitted from knowing that financial worries were a significant stressor for her. Perhaps if she had known this, she may have caught herself before starting to seek solutions through gambling.

Claudine's Story

Claudine was in recovery for several months and was doing all the things she had planned to protect her from relapse. One Thursday evening her father rang her to say he had been made redundant from his job and was very upset. Claudine found herself getting upset and then started to worry about money. Her father had always supported her before. What if he couldn't help her anymore? What would she do? Her mind switched to gambling and how a good win would solve her money worries. She started to go online to open an account.

What we see from this example is that Claudine would have benefitted from knowing that financial worries were a significant stressor for her. Perhaps if she had known this, she may have caught herself before starting to seek solutions through gambling.

List of Top Stressful and Exciting Life Circumstances

Discuss this list with your partner, family, close friend, or support structure. Which of these events are most likely to affect you? Which of them will place you at greater risk of gambling?

Death of a spouse	Change in responsibilities at work
Divorce	Son or daughter leaving home
Marital separation	Trouble with in-laws
Jail term	Outstanding personal achievement
Death of a close family member	Spouse begins or stops work
Personal injury or illness	Begin or end school/college
Marriage	Change in living conditions
Fired at work	Revision of personal habits
Marital reconciliation	Trouble with boss
Retirement	Change in working hours or conditions
Change in health of family member	Change in residence
Pregnancy	Change in school/college
Sex difficulties	Change in recreation
Addition of new family member	Change in church activities
Business readjustment	Change in social activities
Change in financial circumstances	A moderate loan or mortgage
Death of a close friend	Change in sleeping habits
Change to a different line of work	Change in number of family get-togethers
Change in number of arguments with spouse	Change in eating habits
A large mortgage or loan	Holidays
Foreclosure of a mortgage or loan	Christmas
	Minor violations of the law

Turbulence

Take a Minute to Think

Imagine a pilot flying a passenger plane across the ocean. He is relaxed as he is in mid-flight and he has engaged the auto-pilot. He notices that his instruments are telling him that there is bad weather ahead; turbulence is to be expected. What does he do?

A. Nothing
B. Heads to the back of the plane and hides
C. Switches off auto-pilot and takes control

Hopefully, you will have picked (C) as the most likely option. You should act like the pilot when there is turbulence ahead in your life – switch off your automatic functioning and take control. That means doing some things that will increase your chance of negotiating the turbulent time safely.

Life is more complex than flying a plane; there is more to avoid and more turns to be made. It is a lot more like driving a car. Self-driving cars might be possible in the future, but right now they are very dangerous. Running your life on auto-pilot is the same; very risky. You will need your mind to kick in and for you to take control. This is especially true when situations are risky.

High-risk Situations

Turbulence, or a high-risk situation, refers to a time when you feel the urge to slip back to old behaviours. It is specifically these times that you need to plan for and be prepared to meet face-on. Some of the life events discussed above may place you in that situation, or it may be something not contained in that list.

When you have a lapse, it is hard to think clearly; there are lots of negative emotions and thoughts of failure and feelings of guilt. These emotions and thoughts make thinking and deciding difficult. What you need to do is catch hold of yourself, reach out for help, and try not to gamble. We are trying to use foresight here to prevent a lapse rather than hindsight after the damage has occurred.

One way of helping keep yourself safe is to create a personal crisis plan, as described in '**Complete Your Own Personal Crisis Plan**'. A personal crisis plan is like a tool-box for times when things get a bit tricky. It allows you to have a range of options to hand, so you don't have to think before you act to reduce or prevent the risk of the lapse. The plan can be filled in using information gained in Chapter 7 about coping with cravings or Chapter 8 about managing your triggers ('**Managing Triggers**'), or Chapters 10 and 11 about challenging gambling-permissive thoughts and mental traps.

What is important in this task is that you remember those times you have resisted gambling or coped when things were difficult. It is likely you have done some things that helped. Try to recall those things you did; what were they? Who did you call? How did you distract yourself? All difficult times end and sometimes it is just because time passes and you feel better and more in control.

Complete Your Own Personal Crisis Plan

Draw upon your experience of *what works for you*. Use insights learnt in previous chapters and previous times when you successfully resisted gambling.

My Personal Crisis Plan

If I encounter a high-risk situation and feel a strong urge to gamble then I will …

1. _____

2. _____

3. _____

4. _____

5. _____

Safe Places I Could Go if I Am Feeling Vulnerable

1. _____

2. _____

3. _____

These Are the People I Could Contact if I Felt the Urge to Gamble

Name   Phone No.

_____   _____

_____   _____

_____   _____

_____   _____

_____   _____

Riding out a crisis will strengthen my recovery.

I will get through this.

How Family and Friends Can Help

The Personal Crisis Plan above shows that we would recommend calling someone to discuss a crisis. People often find this hard to do because of the fear of upsetting their loved ones and losing any respect and trust they may have gained while not gambling. Yet we know that reaching out is one of the most effective ways to protect yourself during a crisis.

Reactions by friends and family to a lapse or crisis are somewhere on a line that stretches from *Complacency* to *Catastrophe*. Perhaps the better place to be is somewhere in the middle of that line in terms of their reaction to a lapse – that is, they should take it seriously but should not over-react. Identifying significant others whose reactions are more likely to be somewhere in the middle of the continuum and can stand by you may help with your recovery.

While we cannot tell relatives and friends not to be upset, we do try to suggest that they understand that lapses and other crises are a possibility and that they do not mean that the gambling problem has returned. When you are in recovery, you are at risk of returning to gambling, and the way friends and family react will may make it more or less likely that they stop the lapse or relapse back to old behaviours. We strongly recommend that you have a discussion with a relative, carer, or friend about the possibility of lapses and crises. This can reduce some of the fear associated with owning up about a lapse. If you feel that you can 'own' your vulnerabilities about a lapse, they will be much less likely to push you towards gambling.

It can be helpful if both you and your relative/friend/carer see the gambling as a common enemy: an invader in your lives that you both want to get rid of. It promotes recovery to view lapses in this light as it can help channel the upset felt into more positive and helpful reactions from both parties to make further lapses less likely and banish the spectre of any past relapses.

Take a Minute to Think

Make a list of family, friends, and trusted individuals you could include in your long-term recovery. Meet with them and discuss the progress you have made and how they may support you in the future.

Acceptance

Another issue which often undermines longer term progress and recovery is events that are not happening now, but happened years ago. These can include childhood abuse, traumatic events in adulthood, betrayals, and abuse of power. These often cause upset and can affect not only the relationships we form, but also how we think about ourselves. Yet here is the rub: we can never change these things. They have happened and are non-reversible. The only thing we can do is to change how they affect us right now. And in that regard, the first thing that needs doing is *accepting* that it happened. If you have ever been to Gamblers Anonymous (GA), you may have heard the serenity prayer.

Here is a non-religious version I like:

> *Develop the courage to solve the problems that can be solved, the serenity to accept those problems that can't be solved, and the wisdom to know the difference.*
>
> (*The Happiness Trap*, p. 68)

If you are struggling to 'know the difference', we suggest discussing this with a friend, therapist, or sponsor. It is important to know what you can work on right now and what will just have to be accepted. Trying to solve a problem that can't be solved will only frustrate you and keep upsetting memories in the forefront of your mind.

Tariq's Story

Tariq had quit gambling but could not get over the fact that his brother-in-law had 'stolen' his business from him when he was in a crisis five years ago. He was constantly plotting revenge and thought that if he could 'win big' he could start a new business and compete and defeat his brother-in-law. Later he realised that, even if he had the money, competing in business against his brother-in-law would upset his whole family. A harmonious family life was a core value Tariq held. Any sort of revenge would be counter to this value. He also came to accept that he had 'lost' his business because of his own actions (mostly gambling) and that before he could do anything, he had to maintain a stable recovery, so he decided to focus on his recovery and develop professionally, following a new path.

Acceptance is not about leaving things as they are. Where the problem can be solved, it is about action in that direction. It is not passive, but very active and determined. Energy and determination are aimed in the direction of problems that can be solved.

How Long Is the Recovery Period?

People in early recovery are often concerned about how long it will take 'to be completely recovered'. This is understandable because the early phases of recovery are often painful and demanding. It can be helpful to think of recovery in terms of stages.

Stage 1	Stage2	Stage 3
0–3 months	3–12 months	12–24 months

Stage 1 takes most people approximately three months. GA often talk about ninety meetings in ninety days. It requires very active recovery work and a lot of support. In this period, the task is to control thoughts and urges to gamble. It is recommended that this is predominantly achieved by controlling access to money and to gambling facilities. The reason for this is that you will still be in the habit stage – that period where gambling behaviour is reflexive and automatic and responds to certain stimuli reflexively. The main aim in this period is to not gamble while going about your daily routines.

Stage 2 would be the period beyond the breaking of the habitual behaviour leading up to around the first year away from regular gambling. In this period, we would be hoping that people would be retaining some of the external controls that were effective in stage 1 but relaxing slightly in terms of the need for regular vigilance. We would want people to be expanding on activities other than gambling, maybe retaining rewarding behaviours but keeping up with filling the weekly diary with activities that make life more enjoyable. If controls are relaxed, usually by relaxing financial controls, these should be done very cautiously.

Stage 3 is the period from year 1 to year 2. This can be a more difficult period than expected as more often controls have been relaxed or removed and support is less vigilant. People often feel disappointed that their lives haven't become amazingly happy. This makes this a riskier period than the previous two perhaps, with people often feeling disappointed with their recovery. The trick in this stage is to maintain vigilance without being too vigilant, which can be as tricky as it sounds. In many ways the key to maintaining recovery after the first year is to build a life that is re-warding and fulfilling. And that sort of building takes time. There is no other way to do it. But consider how well you are doing if you have gone more than a year of not gambling. It is a great achievement, just don't allow that auto-pilot to start up again.

Skills Practice

- Identify life events that could place you at greater risk of gambling and prepare for how you will deal with them.

- Develop your personal crisis plan to help you with high-risk situations.

- Identify people in your life who could support you when you experience 'turbulence' in your recovery.

- Recognise the events from your past that you have not accepted yet and try to resolve any lingering feelings so you can move on.

Takeaway Points for Affected Significant Others

- Life events, both positive and negative, are very likely to occur.

- These events are likely to cause 'turbulence' and *may* trigger a return to gambling.

- Understand, by talking openly about such events, which are the most risky events.

- Work with your friend or family member to draw up a personal crisis plan and be part of that plan.

14 How Important Others Can Help

Jenny Cousins and Becky Harris

When someone has a problem with gambling, it not only affects them, but also impacts on their loved ones. Both are affected by gambling in different ways, and both want gambling to be out of their lives. Gambling also affects their relationship with each other: and in order to reduce the impact from gambling harm on both the individual and their loved one, there is work that can be done.

In the rest of this book, we have looked at examples of what people who are gambling problematically can do to change their behaviour, as well as some suggestions for family and friends who want to help.

This chapter is written specifically for family and friends. Throughout it, we will refer to the person who is gambling as your 'loved one', for ease of reading.

Your Well-being

If your loved one has experienced a gambling harm, there are lots of different reactions you might have had, but for most people it is stressful and upsetting. People who have been living with high levels of stress and anxiety can become very good at covering up their feelings, and may be so good at doing this that they hardly notice them anymore.

It might seem wrong to think about your own well-being when your loved one is struggling. However, gambling has impacted your life too, and there is a limit to how helpful you can be to anyone if your own needs are not addressed.

Think about the way flight attendants on planes instruct passengers to put on their own oxygen mask first, before helping someone else. In the same way, people who are upset or stressed are not in a good position to support a loved one and therefore need to look after themselves. You cannot pour from an empty cup.

By identifying your feelings, you are starting to acknowledge how gambling has affected you. This is important in your next steps forward alongside your loved one.

You may have been lied to, which can be particularly difficult in an otherwise close relationship. Lying is usually a result of the shame people feel when caught in a gambling loop; they may mistakenly think they can sort things out without telling anyone, or they may feel they are protecting you from having to experience the burden of financial loss.

For you, however, finding out you have been lied to may feel even more painful than the truth that was covered up. Take time to acknowledge the feelings that lying may have evoked to you.

'**Acknowledging Your Feelings**' lists some of the common feelings people describe when their loved one is gambling. See which ones fit for you, or if you have experienced something else which is not listed here.

Acknowledging Your Feelings

Here we have listed some common feelings people describe when their loved one is gambling.

> ➤ Hurt
> ➤ Betrayal
> ➤ Loss and grief
> ➤ Isolation and loneliness
> ➤ Frustration that their loved one cannot just stop
> ➤ Uncertainty
> ➤ Lack of trust
> ➤ Questioning memories and beliefs about the past
> ➤ Anger
> ➤ Guilt
> ➤ Fear for the future
> ➤ A sense of powerlessness
> ➤ Being on constant high alert for signs that gambling has begun again
> ➤ Disbelief that this is happening to you and what it may mean for you and your family's future

---

Which of these feelings have you experienced recently?

_____

_____

_____

_____

_____

Have your felt anything else not mentioned on the list?

_____

_____

_____

_____

_____

Take time to acknowledge these feelings without judging yourself. Being around someone with a gambling problem can be extremely difficult and can have a great impact on your life.

Coping

People have lots of different ways of coping with the impact of a loved one who gambles. There is no right or wrong way, but some may be more helpful for you than others. What works best will probably depend on your own coping style.

There are three main coping styles. These are listed below, with suggestions of things you can do to care for yourself in each case. You may feel that you fit into more than one category, or you might move between them at different times.

Problem Solver
This is your style if you're a practical 'doer' who likes to address problems directly

Suggestions for Self-care Activities
Learn more about mental health problems
Join a family support group and support others alongside yourself
Join a group that is actively engaging with changing policies around the gambling industry and advertising

Keeping Busy
This is your style if you believe in just getting on with it and making the best of things

Suggestions for Self-care Activities
Engage with your wider community groups
Cook something nice
Listen to music that makes you happy
Look after your physical health by keeping active
Try mindfulness or meditation

A Problem Shared
This is your style if you are someone who feels better when you talk your problems through with another person.

Suggestions for Self-care Activities
Meet a friend
Talk to someone on the phone
Call a helpline
Ask your GP about counsellors in your area

Practise Coping Exercises

Depending on your preferred coping style, commit to yourself that you are going to find time to practise activities that could help you manage your feelings about your loved one's gambling problem or support them better.

Coping Styles

Problem solver
Keeping busy
A problem shared

I am going to do the following to help myself cope with the anxiety, worry, and burden I feel from being in this situation:

_____

_____

_____

_____

_____

_____

You may feel resentment for having to practise coping exercises yourself, as understandably you may not feel accountable for the distress caused to you and your family. However, we know that a gambling problem often affects not only the person who is gambling but those around them too, and having ways to cope may be helpful for all of you.

The Roller Coaster

Family members often describe feeling as if they're on a roller coaster. Sometimes they are very hopeful and believe that change is happening; at other times they feel desperate, as though the problem is insurmountable. This is often linked with how family members perceive their loved one's ability to cope with gambling at that moment. They may feel ok when all evidence shows that their loved one is not gambling, but at the same time on high alert in case things go wrong again. This can be exhausting and allows very little room for anything else.

By joining with your loved one and tackling gambling together, you will be better placed to stop both your lives being controlled by it.

The information previously given in this book and the tips that have been shared are ways for you and your partner to get off the roller coaster and begin to create a steadier path forward.

In each chapter of this book you will have seen tips inviting you to form new conversations around gambling that help to create a shared goal. These suggestions are aimed at helping you support your gambling relative in making the changes you both want: while you are not responsible for your loved one's gambling, you can help them with their recovery.

Conversations about Gambling

Generally family members' experiences of talking with their loved one about gambling are that the conversations are difficult, short, and involve feelings that are tricky to navigate. In order for these conversations to become helpful, consider some of the following ideas and techniques.

➤Set a Regular Time Each Week to Talk about Gambling

Regular is the key word here. The more you are able to talk with each other and the more these conversations become a usual part of your life together, the less tricky they will become. Celebrate the successes, talk about rewards, and learn from situations that have been difficult or have resulted in a lapse. It takes practice. The experience of a helpful conversation where both of you are talking about the way forward will give you the confidence to talk more, and reduce the guilt and shame your loved one may experience about gambling.

➤Helpful Conversations Avoid Blaming and Shaming Statements

Conversations need to be framed so that your loved one has the responsibility for whether they gamble or not, but you and your loved one share the responsibility for creating a safe space where support can be asked for, ideas shared, and a plan for the next steps can be created and agreed.

This should not be a one-way street. However, in the early days of stopping, sometimes it may be helpful for you to think about whether something needs to be thought through separately with a supportive other first, before discussing with your loved one.

You and your loved one may need to agree in advance a strategy for stopping the conversation – e.g. getting a drink or going for a quick walk – so that a different focus can be sought if feelings get in the way of a safe and productive discussion.

➤Pace Yourselves

There might be lots of things that you need to address, but if you try to solve everything at once it may quickly become overwhelming. Slow down. Look at the order and content of the chapters in this book as a guide. Think about small, consistent steps rather than one big one.

➤Get Professional Help if Necessary

Sometimes it's too difficult to make these conversations happen by yourself, or you can find yourself getting stuck on the same points and unable to communicate effectively. It can be incredibly supportive so have someone else with you when you talk, to help steer the discussion in the right direction.

Topics to Discuss

- Finances and stimulus control. This means both stopping access to gambling but also protecting your finances and limiting your loved one's access to cash.
- Thinking together about how to reward non-gambling behaviour in a way that works for both of you, and encouraging a new lifestyle to develop.

- Discovering together what helps and what doesn't help when your loved one is experiencing craving. Some loved ones prefer being reminded that the feelings don't last and being offered ideas to distract themselves. Others find a hug and warm encouragement and support helps them at these times.
- Sharing ideas about situations that may be difficult in the future, and coming up with alternatives or ways of coping in advance.
- Talking about whether there is anything that you can do together that means a step forward in developing a different lifestyle.
- Lapse versus relapse. Remember that lapses do often happen on the road to recovery. It's important for both you and your loved one to be able to talk honestly about any slips along the way, and plan together how these will be dealt with if they occur.
- Remembering together that this process takes time, takes practice, and that a key part of moving forward is learning from tricky situations.

Looking After Yourself and Others

It is important to acknowledge that sometimes there can be abuse (both physical and emotional) within relationships affected by gambling. This can be your loved one behaving in violent ways towards you, or you behaving violently towards your loved one.

We understand how frustrating and devastating gambling problems can be, but your well-being and that of your loved one is of utmost importance. If violence of any kind is involved, more care, space, and professional support should be sought for you, your family and your loved one, but it could also include financial, verbal or psychological abuse.

Children can also be very affected by all that gambling brings to families, despite parents trying to protect them. They may notice that less money is available, or that there is a strained atmosphere in their home. They may experience irritability or lack of attention from those that care for them, conversations they are excluded from, or increased arguments between their loved ones. In extreme cases, gambling may result in the loss of essential needs being met, the loss of important relationships (due to separation, divorce, or being abandoned), and the loss of security (both current and in the future).

It can be hard to think that the problems you are trying so hard to deal with are also affecting your children, and it may seem wrong to talk to them about something as adult as gambling. However, it is more reassuring for a child to have something explained to them calmly and factually than to be left to imagine what is going on. Taking the time to talk to them **in an age-appropriate way** about their feelings, explain problem gambling, and describe how you are getting help and support is important, especially for older children and young people. You may wish to discuss this with a professional or someone you trust first, and sometimes children may benefit from extra professional support to help them make sense of their feelings and experiences.

It is also important to ensure that the child in the future understands that they are likely to be at greater risk of developing a gambling problem themselves. They should be careful with engaging in gambling and that if gambling becomes a problem it is key to get professional support quickly.

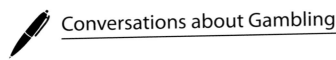

Conversations about Gambling

Initiating conversations with your loved one about their gambling problem can feel like a stressful thing to do, but it is really, really important for the sake of your relationship.

The topics covered in previous chapters in the book could help focus these conversations on certain aspects of gambling.

The following tips could help you have some constructive conversations and prevent conflict:

➤ **Set a Regular Time Each Week to Talk about Gambling**
This is not a one-off conversation. Consistency is really important.

➤ **Helpful Conversations Avoid Blaming and Shaming Statements**
Start your sentences with 'WE' instead of 'YOU'. These conversations are meant to be about how the two of you could work together against gambling, your common enemy.

➤ **Pace Yourselves**
Don't try to deal with everything all at once. Focus on one aspect of the gambling problem each time.

➤ **Get Professional Help if Necessary**
These are difficult conversations so do not hesitate to seek professional help.

Summary

> Changing a gambling habit behaviour takes time. It is your relative's job to stop gambling.

> It is your job to look after yourself and care for those that depend on you.

> It is both of your jobs to create a safe space to talk and support each other so that gambling no longer needs to be a devastating secret that comes between you.

Skills Practice

- Take time to reflect on your own feelings and think about how you can support yourself. This is important and necessary for you to support your loved one, both now and as you move forward.

- Think about whether you need extra support in creating a safe space to talk with your loved one, whether this means talking to someone about your feelings beforehand or getting professional help.

- Practise making gambling conversations a part of your regular routine.

Summary Points for Those Affected by Gambling

- Gambling affects everyone and your family member needs time to reflect on their feelings and what extra support they need in order to be alongside you during your next steps.

- Work with your family member to bring gambling conversations into the open.

- Consider with your loved one the well-being of your entire family, especially if there are children in the family or violence has been a problem.

15 Final Remarks

Venetia Leonidaki and Henrietta Bowden-Jones

We hope that this book has helped you learn more about how to break free from gambling-related harms. If you are reading this book because a loved one is affected, hopefully you now have a better understanding of what it takes for someone to quit their addictive habit. We believe that the strategies presented in this book can be transformative for some people. You will probably have grown tired by now of our reminder that regular practice of the CBT skills found here is necessary before you can experience any benefits. After all, gambling is a powerful habit, and breaking free from it will need plenty of determination and consistent effort.

If you are still having problems breaking free from gambling after having worked with this book, please do not feel disappointed. Self-help books are useful, but a self-help book alone may not be sufficient to help you change your behaviour. This is also true when people try to adopt new healthy habits, such as starting exercise. Many people are able to make exercise part of their daily or weekly routine of their own accord. Watching online videos made by professional trainers acts as the right type of support to get certain people off the couch, whereas others may need to find an exercise class and stick to it in order to feel sufficiently motivated. Finally, for some people, it will take something more drastic, such as regular sessions with a personal trainer, before they get into the habit of exercising regularly. The same idea can be applied dealing with gambling.

If you have tried your best to use this book and have not achieved abstinence or your desired outcome, you may want to consider other sources of help, including professional help. A qualified therapist who has expertise in CBT and ideally works with addictive behaviours could actively guide you to overcome obstacles and put the strategies described here in place. In the UK, clinical or counselling psychologists accredited by the Health and Care Professions Council, or therapists accredited by the British Association for Behavioural and Cognitive Psychotherapies, have the set of skills required to help you with the content of this book. Equivalent accredited bodies exist in other countries. You may even want to bring this book to your initial session with a therapist and ask the therapist if they could help you carry out the exercises. Our appendix also discusses how medication, in addition to talking therapies, may be useful for some people with a gambling disorder.

We would not be surprised to hear that some of our readers were successful in quitting gambling with the help of this book but did not move on to lead a fulfilling life immediately afterwards. It is often only after the gambling is out of the picture that other issues may come to the surface. Indeed, an addiction often acts as an escape and has a numbing effect on painful feelings, such as anxiety or depression. Addictive behaviours also distract us from remembering past traumatic memories and losses. Sometimes people are quick to replace one addictive behaviour with another. Thus, if you feel worse for saying goodbye to gambling, do not be alarmed.

In fact, it's not uncommon for our clients in the clinic to go through a phase of low mood or increased anxiety when they stop gambling. The CBT strategies in this book focus on helping you quit gambling, but your recovery may not necessarily end there. You may have simply completed the first part of your recovery journey before moving towards the next. If you were to seek professional help to address any underlying difficulties, a variety of psychotherapeutic approaches could be helpful, depending on your exact focus. If you would like a therapy to address the deeper roots of your addictive behaviour, psychodynamic therapy may be suitable as an evidence-based treatment for a variety of difficulties. In fact, we have found that psychodynamic therapy has served some of the clients attending our treatment programme very well, especially after the implementation of CBT strategies.

Finally, your relationships may have suffered greatly while you gambled heavily. It would then be entirely understandable if your loved ones felt betrayed or used by you because of your gambling. Coming to the other side of your addictive behaviour could bring increased awareness of how gambling may have hurt your relationships and the work required to repair them and regain their trust. Alternatively, you may have come to realise that a difficult relationship has contributed to your gambling in the first place. In either case, family or couples therapy could be useful, which is the reason for offering it when necessary, as part of our treatment programme, upon completion of a CBT course.

APPENDIX
When to Consider Medication for a Gambling Disorder

Emmert Roberts

This chapter is about how medication, in addition to talking therapies, may be useful for some people with a gambling disorder.

At the time of writing, no medicines were officially licenced for the treatment of gambling disorder. However, lots of research has been conducted on different medications to see if they can help people to reduce or better control their gambling-related disorder. Medicines commonly used to treat depression and anxiety have not been found to have any benefit for people with gambling-disorder; however, a tablet called *naltrexone* has shown promise at helping people reduce the severity of their gambling disorder.

Naltrexone

Naltrexone, also known by its brand names ReVia™ and Vivitrol™, is the only medicine which is currently recommended for the treatment of gambling disorder in international guidelines.

How does naltrexone work?
Naltrexone works by blocking receptors in the brain. Research has shown that two chemical transmitter systems in the brain can be altered in people with gambling disorder. These are the *dopamine* system – which is involved in how people experience reward and pleasure, and the *opioid* system – which is involved in how people experience pain, anxiety, and their mood. Naltrexone blocks certain receptors in the opioid system, and by doing this causes changes in the way messages are transmitted through the opioid and dopamine systems. In some individuals with gambling disorder this blocking action can lead to a reduction in the effects of gambling, a reduction in the desire to gamble, and a reduction in impulsiveness.

How effective is naltrexone at helping with gambling disorder?
A recent study pooled all the available evidence for naltrexone and showed that when people who were receiving talking therapy for gambling disorder were also given naltrexone, there was a greater reduction in their gambling behaviour compared to people who had been given a placebo. However, due to the small number of people taking part in the research there is uncertainty about how large this reduction is. The research to date has also not been able to provide clear answers on what is the best dose of naltrexone for people to take, or for how long people need to be treated with naltrexone. Lots of research is currently being undertaken to try and answer these questions.

What are the side effects of naltrexone?
Nine out of ten people report no side effects when taking naltrexone. For the one in ten people that do experience side effects, the most commonly reported are

stomach upset, headache, drowsiness, and dizziness. All of the side effects are generally mild and typically resolve within one week of starting naltrexone.

Which people with gambling disorder should be considered for naltrexone?

Naltrexone should always be started alongside talking therapy for gambling-disorder. Specialists think about adding naltrexone to someone's talking therapy if:

a) People are not responding as well as hoped to talking therapy and are still struggling with gambling disorder or

b) People have relapsed and started gambling after having completed a set of previous sessions of talking therapy.

Naltrexone may be particularly useful for people who have intense urges to gamble, have lots of family members who also have problems with gambling, or if they struggle to control the amount of alcohol they drink.

Naltrexone cannot be taken by people who have severe liver disease, or by people taking specific tablets or painkillers which contain an 'opioid'. These include medications that contain codeine or morphine. When people start taking naltrexone, they have to state that they are aware they should not take any medication containing an opioid. This includes any medication prescribed by their doctor, any medication bought over the counter, or anything bought illicitly on the street.

How Does It Work in Practice to Get a Prescription and Start Taking Naltrexone?

When naltrexone is used to treat gambling disorder it should only ever be started *by a specialist* at one of the UK's problem gambling clinics and not by a general practitioner.

The following describes the process developed at the National Problem Gambling Clinic (NPGC), and what to expect if you start taking naltrexone.

The Decision to Start Treatment with Naltrexone

The decision to start naltrexone, alongside your talking therapy, should be made collaboratively between you and the gambling specialist. The discussion should include an explanation of how limited the amount of research evidence is for naltrexone, the side-effect profile of naltrexone, the procedure for monitoring while you are on naltrexone, and the fact that while taking naltrexone you cannot take medications that contain an opioid.

Before you start naltrexone, you need to have a blood test to make sure the liver is working correctly, as people with severe liver disease cannot take naltrexone. This blood test is normally organised through your general practitioner, who will feed back the results to the problem gambling specialist clinic.

In some clinics you may also be asked to provide a urine sample to check that there are no medications that contain an opioid in your body before you start to take naltrexone. This practice differs from clinic to clinic, so don't worry if this doesn't happen before you start taking naltrexone.

Once the results of the blood test, and the urine test if you've had one, have been checked, you are ready to start taking naltrexone.

How do I take naltrexone?

Naltrexone comes in small 50 milligram (mg) tablets. When you first start to take naltrexone, you will take half a tablet (25 mg) once a day, at the same time each day, for three days. After those three days you will take a full tablet (50 mg) once a day at the same time each day. You will be given a prescription, that you can fill at any pharmacy, that will last for six weeks.

After six weeks your specialist will ask you to have another blood test with your general practitioner to check the liver and will discuss with you how the last six weeks have been while taking naltrexone. In addition, they will go through any side effects you may have experienced. If there has been no improvement in your gambling disorder at this point, the specialist is likely to recommend stopping the naltrexone and not providing any more. You can have a discussion with the specialist about appropriate next steps in your treatment.

If there has been improvement in your gambling disorder, you and your specialist may decide its appropriate to continue naltrexone treatment and you will be provided with a prescription for a further six weeks at the same dose (50 mg) once a day, to be taken at the same time each day.

You would then have a similar review with your specialist, again with a blood test to check the liver, at the end of this second six-week period. If you continue to show improvement in your gambling behaviour the responsibility for prescribing naltrexone can be transferred to your general practitioner, and they can then continue to issue naltrexone prescriptions for as long as you feel naltrexone is beneficial. Your GP would also conduct the blood test monitoring of your liver every six months while you are taking naltrexone.

Naltrexone and the Future

While current practice at the NPGC is to provide people with a regular dose of 50 mg naltrexone once each day, as further research is conducted, the recommendations about the best dose and how often to take naltrexone may change. Studies are currently looking at whether taking naltrexone 'as required', i.e. taken one to two hours before an anticipated period of gambling, might be a better way for people to use it as opposed to taking it once a day.

Take Away Points

- Naltrexone is the only medicine recommended in international guidelines for the treatment of gambling disorder.
- Naltrexone should always be started by a specialist and started alongside talking therapy.
- People with severe liver disease or those taking medication which contains an opioid cannot take naltrexone.
- Current research shows that naltrexone causes a reduction in gambling behaviour compared to placebo, but research is still ongoing and there is uncertainty about how large a reduction.

A quick guide for the use of naltrexone in a gambling disorder

How does naltrexone work?	Naltrexone blocks receptors in the brain which can lead to people experiencing a reduction in the pleasurable effects of gambling, a reduction in the desire to gamble, and a reduction in impulsiveness.
How good is naltrexone at treating gambling disorder?	Naltrexone causes a reduction in gambling-behaviour compared to placebo, but research is still ongoing and there is uncertainty about how large a reduction.
What are the side effects of naltrexone?	Nine out of ten people experience no side effects. In those who do, common side effects are stomach upset, headache, and dizziness. These tend to be mild and stop within a week.
Who should try naltrexone for gambling disorder?	Naltrexone should always be started alongside talking therapy. Specialists consider naltrexone when talking therapy is not working as well as they hoped for or when people have relapsed after previous talking therapy.
Is there anyone who can't use naltrexone for gambling disorder?	Yes. People with severe liver disease, or those taking any medication that contains an *opioid*.
Can I get naltrexone from any doctor?	No. Naltrexone for gambling disorder has to be prescribed by a specialist in a problem gambling clinic.
Do I need any special tests to take naltrexone?	Yes. You should have a blood test before starting and regular blood tests while taking naltrexone to check the function of your liver.
What dose of naltrexone should I take?	You start taking half a tablet (25 mg) once a day for three days, then take a full tablet (50 mg) once a day thereafter.

References

AFINet-UK & The National Problem Gambling Clinic. (2020). *Gambling, the Family and YOU: A Self-Help Handbook for Family Members* (2nd edn.). Northern Gambling Service.

American Psychiatric Association, DSM-5 Task Force. (2013). *Diagnostic and Statistical Manual of Mental Disorders: DSM-5™* (5th edn.). American Psychiatric Publishing, Inc. https://doi.org/10.1176/appi.books.9780890425596

Anselme, P., Robinson, M. J., & Berridge, K. C. (2013). Reward uncertainty enhances incentive salience attribution as sign-tracking. *Behavioural Brain Research*, *238*, 53–61.

Beck, A. T., Wright, F. D., Newman, C. F., & Liese, B. S. (1993). *Cognitive Therapy of Substance Abuse*. Guilford Press.

Castellani, B., & Rugle, L. (1995). A comparison of pathological gamblers to alcoholics and cocaine misusers on impulsivity, sensation seeking, and craving. *International Journal of the Addictions*, *30*(3), 275–289. https://doi.org/10.3109/10826089509048726

Chen, D., Moskowitz, T., & Shue, K. (2016). Decision-making under the gambler's fallacy: evidence from asylum judges, loan officers, and baseball umpires. *The Quarterly Journal of Economics*, *131*(3), 1181–1242.

Clark, L. (2014). Disordered gambling: the evolving concept of behavioral addiction. *Annals of the New York Academy of Sciences*, *1327*(1), 46.

Clark, L., Boileau, I., & Zack, M. (2019). Neuroimaging of reward mechanisms in Gambling disorder: an integrative review. *Molecular Psychiatry*, *24*(5), 674–693.

Clark, L., Lawrence, A. J., Astley-Jones, F., & Gray, N. (2009). Gambling near-misses enhance motivation to gamble and recruit win-related brain circuitry. *Neuron*, *61*(3), 481–490.

Curry, S., Marlatt, G. A., & Gordon, J. R. (1987). Abstinence violation effect: validation of an attributional construct with smoking cessation. *Journal of Consulting and Clinical Psychology*, *55*, 145–149.

Durrant, R., Adamson, S., Todd, F., & Sellman, D. (2009). Drug use and addiction: evolutionary perspective. *Australian & New Zealand Journal of Psychiatry*, *43*(11), 1049–1056.

Ferris, J., & Wynne, H. (2001). *The Canadian problem gambling index: Final report*. Ottawa: Canadian Centre on Substance Abuse.

Grant, J. E., Brewer, J. A., & Potenza, M. N. (2006). The neurobiology of substance and behavioral addictions. *CNS Spectrums*, *11*(12), 924–930.

Greenberger, D., & Padesky, C. (2015). *Mind Over Mood: Change How You Feel by Changing the Way You Think* (2nd edn.). Guildford Press.

Harris, R. (2011). *The Happiness Trap*. Robinson.

Hodgins, D., & Diskin, K. (2008). Motivational interviewing in the treatment of pathological gambling. In H. Arkowitz, W. Miller, & S. Rollinck (eds.), *Motivational Interviewing in the Treatment of Psychological Problems*. The Guilford Press.

Kim, S., & Lee, D. (2011). Prefrontal cortex and impulsive decision making. *Biological Psychiatry*, *69*(12), 1140–1146.

Kober, H., Mende-Siedlecki, P., Kross, E. F., Weber, J., Mischel, W., Hart, C. L., & Ochsner, K. N. (2010). Prefrontal–striatal pathway underlies cognitive regulation of craving. *Proceedings of the National Academy of Sciences*, *107*(33), 14811–14816.

Martínez-Vispo, C., Martínez, Ú., López-Durán, A., del Rio, E. F., & Becona, E. (2018). Effects of behavioural activation on substance use and depression: a systematic review. *Substance Abuse Treatment, Prevention, and Policy*, *13*, 36.

Meng, Y. J., Deng, W., Wang, H. Y., Guo, W. J., Li, T., Lam, C., & Lin, X. (2014). Reward pathway dysfunction in gambling disorder: a meta-analysis of functional magnetic resonance imaging studies. *Behavioural Brain Research*, *275*, 243–251.

Mentzoni, R. A., Laberg, J. C., Brunborg, G. S., Molde, H., & Pallesen, S. (2014). Type of musical soundtrack affects behavior in gambling. *Journal of Behavioral Addictions*, *3*(2), 102–106.

Miller, W. R., & Rollnick, S. (2013). *Motivational Interviewing: Helping People to Change* (3rd edn.). The Guilford Press.

Orford, J., Cousins. J., Smith, N., & Bowden-Jones, H. (2017). Stress, strain, coping and social support for affected family members attending the National Problem Gambling Clinic, London. *International Gambling Studies*, *17*(*2*), 259–275.

Potenza, M. N. (2013). Neurobiology of gambling behaviors. *Current Opinion in Neurobiology*, *23*(*4*), 660–667.

Presson, P. K., & Benassi, V. A. (1996). Illusion of control: a meta-analytic review. *Journal of Social Behaviour and Personality*, *11*, 493–510.

Raylu, N., & Oei, T. P. S. (2004). The Gambling Related Cognitions Scale (GRCS): development, confirmatory factor validation and psychometric properties. *Addiction*, *99*, 757.

Ryan, F. (2014). *Willpower for Dummies*. John Wiley & Sons.

Sharpe, L., & Tarrier, N. (1992). A cognitive behavioral treatment approach for problem gambling. *Journal of Cognitive Psychotherapy: An International Quarterly*, *6*, 193–203.

Spada, M. M., Caselli, G., Nikčević, A. V., & Wells, A. (2015). Metacognition in addictive behaviors. *Addictive Behaviors*, *44*, 9–15.

Sundali, J., & Croson, R. (2006). Biases in casino betting: the hot hand and the gambler's fallacy. *Judgment and Decision Making*, *1*, 1–12.

Tavares H, Zilberman, M. L., Hodgins, D. C., & el-Guebaly, N. (2005). Comparison of craving between pathological gamblers and alcoholics. *Alcoholism Clinical and Experimental Research*, *29*(*8*), 1427–1431. https://doi.org/10.1097/01 .alc.0000175071.272.98

Van Holst, R. J., Sescousse, G., Janssen, L. K., Janssen, M., Berry, A. S., Jagust, W. J., & Cools, R. (2018). Increased striatal dopamine synthesis capacity in gambling addiction. *Biological Psychiatry*, *83*(*12*), 1036–1043.

Ward, S., Smith, N., & Bowden-Jones, H. (2018). The use of naltrexone in pathological and problem gambling: a UK case series. *Journal of Behavioral Addictions*, *7*, 827–833.

Wareham, J. D., & Potenza, M. N. (2010). Pathological gambling and substance use disorders. *The American Journal of Drug and Alcohol Abuse*, *36*(*5*), 242–247.

Online Resources

www.mindful.org/

www.dummies.com/health/mental-health/ willpower/willpower-for-dummies-cheat-sheet/

www.dummies.com/health/mental-health/ willpower/3-great-online-resources-for-more-willpower-information/

Index